MW00654489

BACK OFF!

Your Kick-Ass Guide to Ending Bullying at Work

105 Practical Tools You Need to Understand, Report, and Effectively End Workplace Bullying

Catherine Mattice, MA
E.G. Sebastian, CPC

All rights reserved. No part of this book shall be reproduced or transmitted in any form or by any means, electronic, mechanical, magnetic, photographic including photocopying, recording or by any information storage and retrieval system, without prior written permission of the publisher. No patent liability is assumed with respect to the use of the information contained herein. Although every precaution has been taken in the preparation of this book, the publisher and author assume no responsibility for errors or omissions. Neither is any liability assumed for damages resulting from the use of the information contained herein.

Copyright © 2012 by Catherine Mattice, MA and E.G. Sebastian, CPC

ISBN 978-0-7414-7682-1

Printed in the United States of America

Published August 2012

INFINITY PUBLISHING
1094 New DeHaven Street, Suite 100
West Conshohocken, PA 19428-2713
Toll-free (877) BUY BOOK
Local Phone (610) 941-9999
Fax (610) 941-9959
Info@buybooksontheweb.com
www.buybooksontheweb.com

More Praise for BACK OFF!

"This book doesn't let you feel like a victim - it forces you to take a look at your situation and yourself, and be a fighter. Back Off! provides clear and tangible action items that you can use to end the bullying."

- Greg S. Reid, Best-selling Author, Speaker, Filmmaker

"If you're looking for a practical, comprehensive resource to empower you to say no to workplace bullying, look no further than Back Off – Your Kick Ass Guide to Ending Bullying at Work. Drawing upon their extensive knowledge and years of hands on experience, Catherine Mattice and E. G Sebastian, have produced a well-organized, easy to read book that will be invaluable to anyone interested in recognizing and responding to workplace bullying. Now everyone can 'choose to be part of the solution,' by taking action to stop workplace bullying."

– Erica Pinsky, Author of Road to Respect: Path to Profit

"Catherine and E.G. have provided a valuable resource for both targets of workplace bullying and managers who need to get a handle on the devastating effects that workplace bullying and mobbing has on all aspects of the organization—which ultimately impacts the bottom line. This well thought out book cuts through the confusion, dispels myths and provides practical and actionable advice for those struggling with bullying at work and those charged with creating humane, respectful, creative and profitable workplaces."

– Anton Hout, OvercomeBullying.org

"BACK OFF! is packed with much needed and refreshing advice that guides targets of workplace bullying through alternative approaches that may just tip the power balance back their way. As important, the book's emphasis on how to proactively communicate desired results provides insight and solutions even for those accused of bullying."

**– Beverly Peterson, Documentary Filmmaker &
Assistant Professor, Montclair State University,
School of Communication & Media**

Table of Contents

"There are two primary choices in life:
to accept conditions as they exist,
or accept the responsibility for changing them."

— Denis Waitley, Author

From the Authors

Knowledge is power.

This book will arm you with the information and guidance you need to successfully navigate your way through the turmoil of dealing with workplace bullying and the managers who may deny your experiences are genuine.

We are realists. This book was written with real research and experience. And the reality is, we aren't going to sugar-coat things for you. This book provides the real facts and real, practical tools you can use to make real change – and end the bullying in your workplace.

No matter what, you are responsible for your own happiness. If the bullying goes on for too long, and you are not receiving the help you need from managers, the damage that can occur to your self-esteem and dignity can be irreparable. The only one who can stop that damage from occurring is you. *You* have to make *your life* better.

Please note that the information in this book is not meant to be a substitute for legal counsel, therapy, or the rules of your own organization. If you need to, please consult an employment law attorney, counselor or therapist.

Note to Readers

As you read this, I will tell you in advance - this was one of the easiest recommendations I have ever written. As a proponent of organizational health, research and personal experience have shown me, "bad managers" and negative employees are the ultimate scourge to the well-being of the individual and to the workplace as a whole. The book you are about to read is <u>not</u> just about inept or mean leadership; rather it addresses an often unspoken evil in many of our workplaces. It is the taboo of "workplace bullies" that has been pushed to the forefront of corporate health in the past decade – and *whether they are in management or not*, they wreak havoc at several levels of the organization.

Defined by Ubanski and S. Permuth (2009), bullying can be described as unprovoked aggression characterized by an imbalance of power where a person who is more physically or emotionally powerful attacks one with less power. It is a repeated behavior intended to harm or disturb another person. Bullying can encompass overt aggressive behaviors or can take more subtle forms. It is notable that this definition was adopted from a book targeted to educators and parents of school-aged children.

The same definition of bullying applies to the workplace as well. Within the past decade, our country has seen workplace bullying rise to the forefront of Human Resource complaints, Ombudsman mediation, corporate blogs, and workplace media; and it has been incorporated into many forward-thinking corporate wellness programs. *Back Off! Your Kick-Ass Guide to Ending Bullying at Work,* as written by Catherine Mattice and E.G. Sebastian, two thought leaders and experts in this field, provides more guidance to businesses and their employees on this critical topic.

This book is so powerful because it explores two key pathways for the individual who is being bullied. The first area of emphasis is on individual personal development and resilience during the period of difficulty at work. The second focus of the book is on specific, tangible instructions for ending the bullying. To my knowledge, this is the only book that provides such detailed information for talking to HR, gaining insight into self-reflection after such meetings, and for forming a plan of action for making necessary change.

At present, much of the workplace bullying paradigm is that targets of bullying have very little chance at rectifying their situation. Catherine and E.G's book goes against this premise. They are saying (and I am saying too) that if you follow their guidance, the chances of getting help from management go up substantially. The targets of workplace bullies really can receive help from mangers, and moving through this evidence-based approach helps cement the betterment of the targeted individual and oftentimes the workplace culture itself.

Finally, I would be remiss if I didn't show my admiration for Catherine and E.G. for writing this book. What a great synergy of minds and expertise! Catherine and E.G. did not write this book as a result of only pure research – they both experienced workplace bullying, and as a result developed a passion for this topic and decided to help others deal effectively with workplace bullying. E.G. has been speaking on conflict in the workplace and bullying (in its many forms) for almost a decade. Catherine is a known expert in the field of workplace bullying internationally, and has been presenting workshops and seminars, and providing consulting to organizations, since 2004.

~Dr. Rachel Permuth

Dr. Rachel Permuth is a nationally-recognized expert in organizational health and workplace strategy. She is delighted to dedicate this to her own workplace bully...

Gratitude to you, Dr. J.B. – for showing me what leadership is *not*. My sincere hope for anyone who has been under your line of supervision is that they can heal and move forward after having dealt with you. It is *you, J, who is in "need of mentorship."*

Foreword

We often hear and read about how bullying has become a major problem in our schools. However, few people recognize that there is another area where bullying has become a serious issue: the workplace. In *Back Off! Your Kick-Ass Guide to Ending Bullying at Work,* Catherine Mattice and E. G. Sebastian shine a light on this growing problem.

I've said for a long time that people who feel good about themselves produce good results, and people who produce good results feel good about themselves—so they want to stay and contribute. There is little doubt that people seldom leave organizations because of compensation. Most often, they leave because of how they are treated by their boss or by people around them.

Perhaps you are reading this book because you believe workplace bullying is happening to you or someone you know. To help you identify what bullying looks like and evaluate the degree to which it may be occurring, the authors have provided an assessment at the front of the book. Whether you need basic advice on standing up for yourself, tips on reporting the behavior to upper management, or real help in knowing when it's ultimately time to move on, this book will empower you to take action. You will also gain a greater understanding of what causes bullying behaviors and learn the psychological and economic impact of bullying on employees and organizations. I've never seen a more comprehensive or valuable handbook on this topic.

Thanks, Catherine and E.G., for helping us learn again that the best way to interact with others is by following the Golden Rule— Treat others as you would like to be treated; or the more recently coined Platinum Rule—Treat others as *they* would like to be treated. Whichever motto you prefer, the important thing to remember is that bullying in the workplace is unacceptable behavior that must be taken seriously. We all need to do what we can to create supportive, caring environments in our workplaces.

~ Ken Blanchard
Chief Spiritual Officer, The Ken Blanchard Companies
Coauthor of *The One Minute Manager*® and
Leading at a Higher Level

Introduction

"Help, I'm the Target of Workplace Bullying!"

"You screwed up again! Can't you count? Get out of my office, you idiot!" As bad as this sounds, John was relieved that Sam, John's personal tormentor, did not toss his stack of documents off his desk, as he had so many times in the past.

John was close to celebrating his one-year anniversary at the company where he works in the warehouse, filling customer orders. There has never been a complaint about John from clients, but Sam, a veteran of twelve years in the department, has been bullying John from his first day on the job. The name-calling and yelling never cease. Sometimes Sam even spills John's coffee on his paperwork or hides documents, forcing John to waste hours of company time re-doing his orders.

When John challenges Sam, Sam just laughs and retorts, "I was just kidding with you; can't you take a joke?" At other times, Sam yells, "Stop wasting my time with this bullsh*t! Go back to work and stay out of my face!"

Sam's behavior is affecting John's every aspect of life. He can't sleep and dreads going into the office; he cannot focus, and his productivity is below 50% of his capability. He has considered talking to upper-management about the daily torment he is facing, but he is afraid that they will blame him for what's going on. Sam has also been at the company much longer than

John, and Sam is definitely great at what he does. Everyone knows Sam is well respected by the managers and even the CEO. Plus, John thinks he should be able to handle any problems with his co-workers without help. Consequently, John feels helpless and desperate. He thinks maybe it's time to start looking for another job, but with the economy the way it is, that seems like a dreadful and risky move. He knows that even if he found another job, there's no guarantee that he wouldn't have to put up with even greater challenges than in his current job. He feels stuck and confused...

John's story shows how workplace bullying is a destructive, life-altering, and emotionally devastating occurrence. People who are bullied live under constant tension, stress, and fear of the bully striking again. And what will the next strike be like?

Living with bullying in your workplace has serious personal consequences, including health problems, such as depression, anxiety, chronic headaches, stomach ailments, and inability to focus; career consequences, such as having to quit a job or give up a lucrative career; and enormous business and financial consequences for the company, including lower productivity, higher healthcare costs, high turnover, and litigation.

We wrote this book for you if you are a target of workplace bullying. You probably heard a million times that "knowledge is power." When it comes to stopping or preventing workplace bullying, some specialized knowledge will definitely save you from unnecessary stress and many sleepless nights. This book will give you an understanding of what is happening, why it is happening, and how to help yourself deal with it effectively.

The information in the following pages should also be useful if you are not directly the target of bullying, but are witnessing bullying among co-workers, or if you are a manager dealing with bullying employees. This book will give you a full picture of the magnitude of damage caused by this behavior, and will provide you with tips on how you can contribute to rectifying some of the madness you are witnessing.

We begin this book with an overview of workplace bullying. In Chapter One, we debunk common misconceptions about bullying at work. Chapter Two is an overview of the types of workplace bullying you might experience, given that bullying behaviors run a continuum of incivility all the way up to violence. Chapter Three will provide you with insight on the common reasons why people behave like bullies.

Chapter Four addresses the very delicate subject of YOU and why you might be the target of bullying. Chapter Five offers powerful tips to end the bullying.

Chapter Six provides insight into reporting bullying to managers in a way that will get their attention. Chapter Seven outlines the psychological and economic impact of bullying on businesses and their most important asset: employees. You will find this information useful as you talk to your supervisors, managers, human resources, and leaders about the destructiveness of your co-worker's behavior.

Our hope is that you will read, use, and share the information we present here so that you can make a real difference in your own life. You can reclaim your life and your career but will have to find the strength of will to take action in order to help yourself, and to reduce the trauma of bullying.

The information in this book will help you END workplace bullying. It is a true self-help guide for anyone involved in a workplace bully situation. Go forth and make change!

Assessment: Are you a target of workplace bullying?

Take this assessment to find out if you are a target of bullying at work. As you read each statement, think about how often the person who is bullying you commits the acts described, and circle the number in the column that best suits your answer. (In the assessment, we use the term co-worker, but please note that the statement could be referring to your manager, supervisor, boss, peer, or subordinate.)

	Rarely or never	About once a month	At least once a week
1. My co-worker insults me, makes offensive remarks about me in front of others, criticizes me in a harsh tone, OR has unpredictable angry outbursts.	1	2	3
2. My co-worker is intimidating with his or her body language by getting in my personal space, shoving me, OR staring me down during one-on-one conversations or staff meetings.	1	2	3
3. My superior makes threats about terminating my employment or demoting me, OR tells management that my performance is not good without providing me with information about how to improve.	1	2	3

		1	2	3
4.	Reasoning with my co-worker is like reasoning with a wall; he or she is stubborn, argumentative, and refuses to see other points of view.	1	2	3
5.	My co-worker attempts to isolate me by not inviting me to social events, leaving me out of staff meetings, OR telling others not to be friends with me.	1	2	3
6.	My co-worker spreads rumors and gossip about me.	1	2	3
7.	My co-worker consistently reminds me of mistakes that I have made in the past, makes a big deal out of little mistakes or mishaps, OR accuses me of mistakes that I didn't make.	1	2	3
8.	My co-worker rolls his or her eyes when I talk, OR makes snide comments about how stupid my ideas are in front of others.	1	2	3
9.	My co-worker plays harsh practical jokes on me.	1	2	3
10.	My co-worker makes comments about how worthless or incompetent I am, OR makes comments about how others do not value my contribution to the workplace.	1	2	3
11.	My co-worker withholds information from me that I need to do my job, including things like memos, staff meeting invites, or teleconferences with clients.	1	2	3

12. My co-worker takes away responsibilities that are important to my job; asks me to do things that are far below my level of experience/expertise; assigns me responsibilities that are far above my level of experience/expertise; OR gives me impossible deadlines that no one could meet.	1	2	3
13. My co-worker is an excessive micromanager, asks me to write down everything I do during the day, is untrusting of my capabilities, OR changes my responsibilities or deadlines frequently and without good reason.	1	2	3
14. My co-worker does not allow me to take sick leave or vacation, even when I have earned it.	1	2	3
15. My co-worker takes credit for my work, OR tells others that my ideas were actually his or hers.	1	2	3
16. My co-worker seems to punish me and others at random, such as yelling at some for being two minutes late and not at others for being 30 minutes late.	1	2	3

Total your score: _____

If your score ranges from 16-20: The person you work with might be a bit of a jerk, but he or she is probably just lacking some communication skills. This book will provide you with the information you need to assertively stand up for yourself and get the person to stop treating you with disrespect.

If your score ranges from 21-28: You are working with someone who teeters on workplace bullying behaviors. This book will provide you with an understanding of why your co-worker or manager acts that way, and give you tools to assertively stand up for yourself and report the behavior to management.

If your score ranges from 29-48: You are definitely working with someone who exhibits workplace bullying. This book will provide you with an understanding of why your co-worker or manager acts that way, and give you tools to assertively stand up for yourself and report the behavior to management. If, after implementing the tools you learn in the book, your situation does not change, consider the importance of your health and find a new job.

Please note that only you really know your experiences and how they make you feel. This assessment is simply meant to serve as a guide. No matter what your score, if you **feel bullied, abused, or disrespected at work, then no one can you tell you otherwise (and this book is for you).*

105 Tools at a Glance

Thirteen myths about workplace bullying debunked

#1: There is no such thing as "workplace bullying"

#2: Bullying is no big deal

#3: Bullying is just a personality conflict between two people

#4: Targets have a performance issue and are accusing their boss of being too tough

#5: As grown-ups. everyone should be able to deal with a bully

#6: Targets of bullying are helpless to stop it

#7: It is the targets who "invite" bullying into their lives – it is their fault they are bullied

#8: Targets of bullying are weak

#9: All bullies are evil people

#10: Workplace bullies are nothing more than assertive managers or coworkers

#11: Bullying is just media hype

#12: Bullying targets are protected under harassment and hostile work environment laws

#13: Bullying can be resolved with an anti-bully corporate policy

Six concepts central to bullying

#1: Bullying is recurring, perpetual, and ongoing

#2: Bullying escalates in frequency and level of aggression over time

#3: Bullying causes psychological harm to targets and witnesses

#4: Bullying is about power

#5: Bullying causes communication breakdown among employees and managers

#6: Organizational goals cannot be met when there's a bully, and the bottom line suffers

Five levels of aggression

#1: Incivility
#2: Emotional Bullying
#3: Predatory Bullying
#4: Mobbing
#5: Violence

Eleven reasons people bully at work

#1: Feelings of insecurity
#2: Lacking resourcefulness
#3: Feeling all-powerful or powerless
#4: Lacking effective communication skills
#5: Lacking leadership skills
#6: Easily provoked or have a low tolerance for stressful situations
#7: Have a belief system that supports bullying as acceptable behavior
#8: Personality disorder
#9: Personality style clashes
#10: People who witness the behavior do not stand up to the bully
#11: Your workplace has a bully-friendly work environment or culture

Eleven reasons you might be targeted

#1: Insensitivity and intolerance of "different"
#2: Someone thinks you make too many mistakes or are an underperformer
#3: Someone thinks he or she can get away with being aggressive with you
#4: You stand out with superior knowledge or as a top performer

#5: You are likeable

#6: You come across as shy or unassertive

#7: You are perceived as a complainer

#8: You are a whistleblower

#9: You are dealing with past experiences or present happenings

#10: You have rationalized your co-worker's behavior as acceptable

#11: You are in a new job

Twenty-three tools to end bullying

#1: Acknowledge and name the problem

#2: Confront the person bullying you

#3: Avoid name-calling

#4: Focus on yourself and your actions, not on the bullying

#5: Take control of your response to the bullying behavior

#6: Reframe the situation

#7: Build up your confidence

#8: Focus on building up your self-esteem

#9: Maintain conscious awareness of your body language at all times

#10: Be aware of your conflict management style

#11: Avoid passive language

#12: Use the three steps of assertiveness

#13: Use "You" language

#14: Deflect criticism

#15: Use the tools of DISC

#16: Learn about and practice resilience and optimism

#17: See a doctor and keep documentation regarding your health

#18: Enlist support from friends, family, superiors and co-workers

#19: Stay away from social media

#20: Take care of you

#21: Open your mind to new opportunities

#22: Prepare for job interviews

#23: Take legal action

Four types of manager reactions to bullying complaints

#1: The empathetic manager

#2: The well-meaning manager

#3: The indifferent manager

#4: The cynical manager

Seven must-do's before filing a grievance

#1: Document the workplace bullying

#2: Seek confirmation that you are a good employee and high-performer

#3: Address poor performance evaluations

#4: Determine costs to the organization

#5: Attempt to resolve the issue yourself

#6: Get prepared for the conversation

#7: Self-reflect

Seven solutions to offer your managers

#1: Build a more collaborative and positive workplace

#2: Implement an anti-bullying, or healthy workplace, corporate policy

#3: Seek transfer to a new department or work group

#4: Implement a 360-degree employee review process

#5: Get coaching or training programs

#6: Create a respectful workplace team

#7: Implement an anonymous reporting tool

Eighteen ways bullies wreak havoc on targets and organizations

#1: Pertinent information withheld from – or wrong information given to – targets that prevent them from doing their job effectively and efficiently

#2: Lost customers who were victimized by the bully

#3: Lost customers who heard about the bully from unhappy former customers

#4: Anger management, communication, leadership and other types of training

#5: Increased presenteeism, absenteeism and turnover; unemployment insurance

#6: Increased health insurance costs and workers' compensation

#7: Bad reputation in the industry and business community

#8: Decreased shareholder returns

#9: Legal costs for counsel, litigation, and settlement fees

#10: Loss of motivation and energy

#11: Stress induced psychological and physical illness

#12: Decreased work quality and quantity; decreased employee performance

#13: Lost innovation and ability to learn

#14: Counterproductive workplace behavior

#15: Time spent by co-workers and managers calming and counseling targets, or gossiping about the behavior

#16: Time spent by management appeasing, counseling or disciplining bullies

#17: Time spent reorganizing departments and teams

#18: Time spent by targets looking for different work

CHAPTER 1: KNOWLEDGE IS POWER

Thirteen myths about workplace
bullying debunked

After four years of employment at a large organization headquartered in Los Angeles, Cathy was promoted into the compliance department. The company was doing business in 48 states, and Cathy was responsible for putting together the lengthy renewal applications. Her job was to assemble long answers about the company's business practices, gather the supporting documents, and attach them all to the license renewal forms for each state. Each application took her several weeks to put together. If she made mistakes, the company could lose its license in any of the states in which it was conducting business. Getting promoted into this position meant the leadership team felt Cathy was thorough, detail oriented, and smart enough to handle her responsibilities. And she did handle them—really well in fact. After a few months, she learned that because she had such special knowledge of the company through her information gathering and interviews with managers and leaders, she could make recommendations for improvement to managers about their departments.

At first, Cathy's new boss just seemed to be in a bad mood once in a while. Every now and then Cathy's boss would snap at her or talk down to her, but Cathy just chalked it up to stress or even her own hypersensitivity. Over time, however, the rudeness and snide comments came more frequently, and Cathy began to feel herself getting more and more frustrated with her boss. After a year, Cathy was getting yelled at all of the time, receiving scathing emails almost daily, and often punished for minor errors. Several times, Cathy had even been verbally attacked for being just a minute or two late to work.

After a few years of this kind of abuse, Cathy found out that her boss was also taking credit for her ideas. The president of the organization had learned of several new processes in the compliance department that Cathy had put in place, and members of the leadership team had all applauded Cathy's boss for the good work. Not long after, Cathy received her annual employment review from her boss, and despite four years of great reviews and what she thought was a great job, her boss had nothing but bad things to say. According to the evaluation, which Cathy's boss coerced her into signing, Cathy was insubordinate, showed no initiative, lacked the detail required to do her job well, and was being recommended for a demotion. Needless to say, Cathy was furious.

At this juncture, Cathy had four options: She could accept the demotion and hope things got better; she could go above her boss' head and see if another manager would help her; she could quit; or she could fight back. And after several years of complaining to her friends and family, she decided she'd had enough, and it was time to fight back. Cathy was going to take back her dignity. She gave herself six months to turn things around, and if her efforts didn't work, she was going to quit and go somewhere where she was respected.

Cathy's first step was to realize that she played some part in what had happened to her. Other people in her department were not treated the same way, so she had to wonder what she had done to allow the bullying to get to this point. She kept thinking back to those first few times that she had been mistreated, and wondered what would have been different if she had said something then. Probably a lot. But, Cathy realized she couldn't change the past, and decided to focus on the present and her future.

After three years of complaining to her husband about another day at work with her bullying boss, Cathy made the decision to stop focusing on her unhappiness and the abuse. Focusing on the boss gave the boss power over her—she had allowed her boss to take over her thoughts and allowed her workplace to take over her life. Even when she wasn't at work, Cathy was dealing with the bullying, running the abusive scenarios over and over in her mind. She finally made the conscious decision not to let that happen anymore. She told her husband that if she started to talk about her boss, he was to cut her off and remind her that "the boss was not invited to dinner."

Cathy began to realize that she had been acting like a victim, and that this was not going to help her overcome the problems she faced at work. She realized that the constant yelling, frequent criticism of her work, and the negative evaluations had gotten to her self-esteem, and she needed to rebuild it. Cathy began to read books about building resilience and regaining confidence. She tore down the sign she'd hung over her alarm clock with the words, "Get up!" on them, and replaced it with a sign that said, "You can do it!" She knew it would help her garner the power to get out of bed every morning. On her mirror, she hung another sign that said, "You are better than this. You can do this. You are in charge. You are awesome at your job." These were her positive affirmations— and she kept another copy in the car to look at as she drove to work.

After a few weeks of daily affirmations and some role-playing with her husband and friends, Cathy worked up the nerve to stand up for herself. Standing up for herself did not mean yelling back, but it did mean becoming more assertive. When the boss made comments that were unacceptable to Cathy, she called her boss on them by saying something like, *"Please don't raise your voice at me. It's unnecessary."* The boss would respond by puckering her lips and making a sour face, but at least she would stop yelling.

Cathy also found that when the boss had something to say about Cathy's performance, Cathy could counter by calmly saying things like, *"I understand you are mad because I was a few minutes late, but yesterday I worked until 11:00 pm to be sure I finished the application that needs to go out today. Perhaps we can schedule a quick five minute meeting today to talk about my workload and priorities so that I am sure to work the hours you need."* Cathy was always sure to monitor her body language during these conversations, and she began to focus on standing up straight, keeping her shoulders back, hands on her hips, and eyes locked on her boss when she talked to her. She realized in the process that she'd been hunching over for the last three years! Her back even hurt a little as she forced herself to sit up and stand with her shoulders back at all times.

Cathy's next move was to approach her boss about the nasty employee evaluation she'd received. She sent her boss an email, so that she'd have a record, requesting that they meet to review the evaluation and the next steps. At first, the email was ignored, but after several others over the next few weeks, the last two of which were copied to the human resources department, the boss finally agreed to meet. Before the meeting, Cathy prepared a list of all of the things she had done well, all of the ideas that had been implemented (that the boss had taken credit for), and her goals for improvement over the next six months. The conversation was an uncomfortable one, but Cathy stood her ground. Cathy relayed everything she'd written in her notes about her performance, and asked her bullying boss for details about her negative review. The boss refused to give any, and failed to help Cathy set goals for future performance, as a good manager should do. The meeting was a bust—a waste of time—but she left the meeting with a sense of elation for being able to stand up to her bully.

Cathy then contacted her boss' boss, a vice-president, in order to be sure no one else was taking credit for her ideas, and to talk about the negative evaluation. Cathy did not go into this conversation with the desire to "tattle-tell" or point fingers at her immediate boss. She did, however, want to be sure that she received credit for her ideas and that the vice-president knew she'd tried to work things out. During this conversation, Cathy was sure to discuss her bullying boss in terms of the boss' behavior. She never, ever, said anything like, "She makes me feel awful and she treats me really badly." Cathy focused on the facts, and was sure to say things like, "Here are four emails I received from my boss last week, and I'm sure you will agree that they are quite unprofessional."

She showed the vice-president her negative review, along with the many emails she'd sent requesting a meeting. She told the vice-president about her ideas and the things she'd implemented for which her boss had taken credit. She talked about the fact that she often worked ten and twelve-hour days, but that she'd been verbally attacked and yelled at for being even just a few minutes late. The meeting went well, and the vice-president seemed to take in everything Cathy said. He agreed that Cathy was to come to him with her ideas for new processes so that her boss couldn't claim them as her own. He also agreed to talk with Cathy's boss about her behavior and address the employee evaluation.

Cathy felt relieved after the meeting. She thought things would get better, and they did, for about two weeks. Unfortunately, Cathy's meeting with the vice-president irritated her boss and the abuse started again—but this time, it was worse. Cathy held strong—ensuring that her body language projected confidence, and that she assertively stood up for herself when she was verbally attacked. She was also aware of how she talked to herself—never allowing herself to give in to negative self-talk or slip back into a victim mentality.

Cathy also began to keep a journal of every abusive interaction with her boss. She saved emails, wrote down the details when the boss yelled or berated her, and even saw a doctor about her stress levels. Despite all of her efforts to remain focused on overcoming her bullying boss, she was still extremely stressed out and feeling extraordinarily defeated.

As she neared the six-month mark, Cathy made an appointment with her boss to discuss their working relationship. She also requested that a representative from human resources be there, along with the vice-president she'd spoken to previously. The goal of this meeting was to expose her boss and gain agreement from all three guests that things would change. She knew that if she didn't get that, she was prepared to leave. Quitting would make things tough on her and her husband, but they both agreed her health was worth far more than a paycheck.

Armed with three copies of her journal of facts (not emotions), the abusive emails, doctor's notes about her stress, and a whole lot of courage, Cathy entered the conference room where everyone sat waiting. Over the course of the two-hour meeting, Cathy laid out a timeline of behaviors, idea stealing, manipulation, and psychological abuse. She supported each and every claim by handing the vice-president and the human resources rep a copy of some document, email, or journal entry that supported her claim. Cathy never referred to herself as a victim, and with the exception of the doctor's notes regarding stress, she never talked about her feelings. If she did so, she would be seen as a whiner, a complainer—an employee who can't carry her workload. Everything she said focused on the behaviors of her bullying boss, and the proof was in the pudding—everyone saw that the boss' behavior had gotten way out of hand.

The bullying boss was shocked. She was surprised at the piles of evidence lying before her on the table. The VP couldn't believe this had happened. The human resources rep knew that this needed to end. Together, the four of them laid out a plan of action to ensure that it did. Lucky for Cathy, her managers understood the severity of the problem.

The company immediately hired a communication consultant to help the bullying boss change her ways. They hired an expert in workplace bullying and strategic culture change to develop a corporate policy. They began running company-wide awareness training and management training for spotting bullying and handling grievances. Because of Cathy, the company focused on developing a healthy workplace culture.

Cathy acted smart, but luck was on her side as well. Cathy was lucky that she worked for a company where leadership was committed to providing a safe work environment for everyone. Things definitely could have gone very differently for her, and she may have had to leave the company per the agreement she'd made with herself. She knew that her pride and dignity were not worth the paycheck she received every two weeks—peace of mind, happiness, and self-esteem are priceless.

Cathy's smart actions included the following:

- After those three long years of abuse, she made a decision not to be a victim anymore.
- She started taking responsibility for her own well-being and happiness.
- After doing some research on workplace bullying and resilience, she knew she had to make a change in her attitude and her situation.
- She stopped focusing on how bad she felt and started focusing on the facts.
- She stopped allowing herself to be criticized and belittled and started focusing on assertiveness and projecting confidence with her body language.

While Cathy's story is an inspiration, for many, things don't turn out this way. Many people throughout the world have developed chronic anxiety, depression, and other such symptoms as a result of their situations at work. Some have even taken their own lives because of a bully at work, and because they didn't see any way out of their "trap." Cathy's story is not at all that uncommon, but unfortunately most people—just like Cathy—do not realize that they are being bullied until it's too late.

This book will help you, a target of bullying, recognize early signs before you sink to the point of no return. Cathy could have perhaps put an end to the bullying had she recognized the signs and addressed her boss' behavior early on. We want you to be able to recognize bullying behaviors as soon as they surface. We want you to understand your situation and see it as one with options. You do have a choice, and you do have the power to change what's happening every day at work. After reading this book, we hope you will do what Cathy did and find the strength within yourself to overcome this adverse situation. Ultimately, if your circumstances do not improve, we hope you will search your soul for the courage to leave your organization and find a new place to work.

This book will provide you with the information you need to get the bully to BACK OFF! Read each chapter carefully, and take action.

Before we explore workplace bullying and how to deal with it, it is important to clear up any misunderstandings you or others might have about it. In the case of workplace bullying, knowledge is power.

#1: There is no such thing as "workplace bullying"

When we think about "bullying," most of us think about the schoolyard and not about the workplace. However, workplace bullying is very real, and its destructive effects are also very real.

Heinz Leymann, a social scientist from Sweden, was the first to document abusive behaviors in adults at work. He and a colleague, Bo-Göran Gustavsson, published the first ever article on psychological violence at work in a peer-reviewed scientific journal in 1984. Since then, Leymann has published several research articles on the topic, the most popular of which was his first paper in English, published in another scientific journal called *Violence and Victims* in 1990. Leymann is credited as the forefather of research on workplace bullying, and was the first to notice that it can result in Post-Traumatic Stress Disorder and even in suicide. Since the publication of his articles, *thousands of research studies* on aggressive and bullying behaviors at work have been conducted around the world—documenting how widespread, common, and damaging they are.

Should anyone try to tell you that you are not being bullied because, in their mind, that's not something that happens to adults at work, tell them that 20+ years of research on workplace bullying says otherwise. Some research has indicated that 50% of the population is bullied (e.g., Rayner, 1997), and in some cases even as much as 75% (e.g., Einarsen & Raknes, 1997).

Workplace bullying is real

Thousands of research studies on aggressive and bullying behaviors at work have been conducted around the world, documenting how widespread, common, and damaging they are.

The National Institute for Occupational Safety and Health (NIOSH), found in their study that almost 25% of American businesses have some level of bullying happening in their workplace. This study also found that 11% of the bullying incidents were committed against customers (Blosser, 2004).

CareerBuilder.com, a major job search engine, found in their recent survey of over 5,600 people that one in four people is bullied at work (Grasz, 2011).

The Workplace Bullying Institute, who conducted a study with Zogby International in 2007 and again in 2010, found that 35% of the American workforce is bullied, and an additional 15% have witnessed bullying against a co-worker in the past. That means, according to their studies, 50% of the workforce has been exposed to workplace bullying. Their studies also found that bullying is four times more prevalent than illegal forms of discrimination or harassment (bullying is not illegal, by the way).

The Employment Law Alliance, a group of 3,000 attorneys from around the world, found in their survey that nearly 45% of

American workers have been bullied during their careers (Hirschfeld, 2007).

Finally, in the Corporate Leavers Survey, a survey conducted by an organization called the Level Playing Field Institute, a nonprofit that focuses on fairness in the workplace, 74% of respondents indicated they had been bullied at a former employer's, and 71% indicated they had also been publicly humiliated (2007).

All of these numbers point to one thing: *bullying at work is real and widespread.*

#2: Bullying is no big deal

Independent research in the United States and from around the world has associated bullying with many psychological health problems, including feeling helpless, decreased self-esteem, poor morale, feelings of inadequacy, depression, and development of conflict with co-workers and family members as a result of what's happening at work.

> **Get Help**
>
> If you are thinking about suicide, help is available to you. Work is not worth your life.
>
> National Suicide Prevention Hotline: 1-800-273-TALK (8255) www.suicidepreventionlifeline.org
>
> This is a free, 24-hour hotline available no matter where you live in the United States.

In Leymann's 1990 article, for example, he identified several effects of bullying, including feelings of isolation, desperation, helplessness, rage, anxiety, despair, hyperactivity, and immune system deficiencies. He also estimated in the article that between

100 and 300 people commit suicide each year (in Sweden) as a result of the abuse they experience at work.

Suicides related to bullying at work do not seem to be very prevalent in the media in the United States, but documentarian Beverly Peterson (http://OurBullyPulpit.org) has looked into this issue through the lens of her camera.

US researchers Tracy, Lutgen-Sandvik, and Alberts (2006) found targets likened bullying to being beaten, physically abused, "assassinated," "maimed," "killed," "annihilated," and "raped."

The long-term impact of bullying has also been studied by researchers Matthiesen and Einarsen, who found Post Traumatic Stress Disorder in nearly 77% of their research participants who were bullied (2004). Post Traumatic Stress Disorder is commonly known as PTSD and is a psychological trauma resulting in sleepless nights and severe anxiety, to name only a few of the symptoms. PTSD is also commonly associated with soldiers who return from war.

All of this points to one thing: *bullying is a big deal, and it hurts.*

#3: Bullying is just a personality conflict between two people

A personality conflict occurs when two people disagree on how to handle an unhappy client or what new office furniture to buy; it affects primarily—and at times exclusively—those two individuals. Bullying, on the other hand, affects the employees, co-workers, the workplace, and its leaders.

Bullying is a systemic problem that the entire organization is responsible for allowing to develop, and thus responsible for eliminating. For one, when bystanders witness an incident of workplace bullying, the chances of them standing up for the target are slim. They might also experience psychological fear themselves, asking, "Will I be next?!"

Managers are the ones whose primary responsibility should be to help targets, and for creating an environment where disrespect is not allowed. Unfortunately, most of the time managers do nothing to help—or they are the ones bullying employees—hence targets and bystanders lose respect for them and this drives down quality of work. To create a healthy work environment, managers need the direction and support of the organization's top leaders.

In one author's case, despite the crying, begging, and pleading of employees to the company president that he address bullying behaviors in one particular individual—who was causing major turnover, bottlenecking of information, and upset employees and even customers—the president would not lift a finger. The answer was always, "That's just how he is," "Just let Nick be Nick," or "Why can't you be the

Bystanders

Some bystanders may ignore the bullying altogether, or choose not to pay attention to it. Others may join the "side" of targets and spend time during the work day counseling or consoling them, while others join the "side" of the bully, and may encourage the negative behaviors or even join in.

That means that aggressive people are essentially "allowed" to rise to the top of the social circle because the work community allows it—by not saying anything.

bigger person and just let it go?" The company president never spoke to Nick, the manager who mistreated everyone else in the office.

By failing to respond to a workplace bullying situation, the company president condoned bullying behavior and created a reputation for being tolerant of bullying. Many employees left the organization as a result of the challenging workplace relationships. Other employees chose a different route and became abusive themselves because they'd learned it was okay, and perhaps even expected to behave like a jerk. Hey, if this guy did it and got away with it why shouldn't they?

#4: Targets have a performance issue and are accusing their boss of being too tough

Unfortunately, this is the belief of many human resources managers who refuse to see what's really happening, or don't understand the nature of workplace bullying. People who are bullied often do not have a performance issue at all—in fact, many of them are top performers being singled out by a person who is jealous of their capabilities or threatened by the attention they receive from management for a job well done.

Other times targets have worked in an organization for many years with rave reviews, and when a new boss comes on board, who doesn't know as much about the company as the long-time employee, the reaction is to push the long-time employee down by accusing him or her of being a poor performer. These targets face some of the most difficult situations because they feel more trapped at their workplace than any other target—they've worked at the same company for twenty years! Now what are they supposed to do with a bullying boss and no support from management? For these people, leaving is definitely not an option, but many are forced into early retirement.

We would be lying if we said targets of workplace bullying are never poor performers; there may be instances where that is indeed the case. But, there is an appropriate and effective way to deal with poor performance, and there is an unacceptable, ineffective and bullying way to deal with poor performance. Good bosses who have the respect of their subordinates talk about performance with their employees openly. They find out why performance is low, what training and resources are needed to bring performance up, and set goals for increasing performance and eliminating the problem behaviors. Bullying bosses, on the other hand, just yell and become frustrated easily when someone isn't performing up to their standards. This is ineffective and not beneficial for anyone, including the company.

Performance (mis)management at a community college

Shirley worked at a local community college for twenty-two years. During that time, she received great performance reviews, regular raises, and praise from manager after manager about her work. When there was some re-organization within the college, Shirley found herself reporting to Jennifer, a newly hired department chair.

Jennifer was rude and belittling from the beginning. Emails were curt, and she often accused Shirley of not knowing what she was doing. Shirley also received several performance reviews from Jennifer claiming that her performance was unsatisfactory.

Shirley brought copies of all twenty-two years worth of good evaluations, and Jennifer's two poor evaluations, to the human resources department. She pointed out that the correlation between poor performance and manager change was pretty clear, and provided copies of all of Jennifer's abusive emails.

After filing several complaints against Jennifer, Shirley was finally transferred to a new department. Although safe from the bullying, her new position included a pay cut. Jennifer, left to run the department Shirley had been a part of for twenty-two years, was never reprimanded. This is an example of poor performance management, and while we should praise human resources for at least taking some action to help Shirley—unfortunately, they took unfair action.

#5: As grown-ups, everyone should be able to deal with a bully

The fact is that many targets don't realize that they are being bullied until it gets out of hand. Unlike sexual harassment, racism, or discrimination based on religion or nationality, which have clear laws against them, bullying is not always detected instantly. It's easier to know when you are being sexually harassed or discriminated against because it's more clear-cut and because laws against these behaviors are quickly enforced. For example, you know when you are sexually harassed when you are touched inappropriately or a sexual comment is made, and your human resources manager will know that what you describe is against the law. (And even these behaviors can, at times, be hard to prove.)

Bullying, however, is more subtle and can start with seemingly harmless remarks disguised as jokes; they may escalate into some gossip behind the back of the target; passing around some "funny" emails; poking "fun" at the expense of the target; and occasional yelling. In the beginning, all of this might be overlooked as the target disregards the behavior for various reasons and chooses to focus on work, rather than on giving merit to childish behaviors. After awhile, the target begins to realize that things have gotten out of hand and that they feel awful. And, because bullying is such a new concept for many, they often don't have the words to describe to themselves or others what's happening. They just know that they are under tremendous stress, but it's hard for them to grasp that they are working with someone behaving so childishly or identify that they are being bullied.

In a perfect world, all grown-ups would learn to treat each other with respect and communicate in a healthy way with others. It would be nice if we didn't have to deal with bullies at all, then we wouldn't have to worry about standing up to them.

We all have different levels of tolerance when it comes to disrespect. Some will stand up right away against the smallest infraction against them, while others are more avoidant of conflict, and hence will tolerate negative behaviors in order to avoid confrontation.

The question shouldn't be whether adults can stand up to a bully, but rather, why don't we all act like adults?

#6: Targets of bullying are helpless to stop it

This is a very important myth to challenge. Workplace bullying is a dynamic situation between a person exhibiting bullying behaviors, the target of those behaviors, and the organization as a whole. In no way are we blaming targets or trying to make targets feel guilty, but the high-pressure environment created by workplace bullying often creates a situation where the target potentially exacerbates the situation.

As professionals who work with both targets of bullying behavior and those who commit those crimes, we know that we are walking a fine line here. It is important to debunk this myth that targets are pure victims in order to open up a pathway to change for you. If a target of bullying is not able to take any responsibility for the situation, then the target is reduced to absorbing the abuse, seeking revenge, or leaving the situation. The same holds true for the bully and the employer—they too must take responsibility. If we cannot work on developing new behaviors for both targets and perpetrators,

> If you are not able to take any responsibility for the situation at all, then you are left with no options but to simply take the abuse, seek revenge, or leave the workplace.

and on finding ways to help the organization reward positive behaviors, then we have few helpful options and nothing changes.

Think about it this way: It would be impossible to say that during a conversation with anyone, whether a bully or a nice co-worker, you play no part in the outcome of that conversation. That means you do have some control over the result, and this is a good thing.

#7: It is the targets who "invite" bullying into their lives—it is their fault they are bullied

Many believe that a person is bullied because of a certain personality type or attitude that triggers bullying in others. If this were true, it would imply that there are bullies on the prowl waiting for pray to show up. Last time we checked, we belong to the species of Homo Sapiens, not some wild, cannibalistic predatory class.

Yes, some people do come across as more timid, shy, or of lower confidence, but that does not justify any attack against them, and it certainly shouldn't ignite bullying behaviors in other people. Bullying behaviors stem from ineffective communication skills and a lack of empathy.

#8: Targets of bullying are weak

More often than not, people who are targeted by bullies are individuals who try to put in an honest day's worth of work and who want to get along with others. Their only "weakness" might be their lack of belligerent tendencies.

The real weak people are the bullies who hide their inadequacies and try to seem more powerful by hurting others. There's nothing noble, great, or worthy about people who bully; they are the weak ones.

#9: All bullies are evil people

At first thought, this might seem very much like your situation—it often does seem that bullies are purposeful and intentionally hurtful. It also makes for "juicier" media coverage when a person intentionally hurts another and drives them to insanity for fun or to feel superior. In fact, a lot of people out there are claiming that bullies are psychopaths and sociopaths who can be compared to the mask-wearing Michael Meyers in the series of Halloween movies. And, we know the fear you experience at work might seem comparable to Laurie Strode, the babysitter Michael is intent on stalking until successfully ending her life.

But, we can assure you that research does NOT support the idea that bullying is always intentional and malicious, or that all abusive people at work are psychopaths out for blood. There are times when a highly driven manager or coworker is perceived as pushy or even bullying, but in that person's mind, there's no trace of malice or intent to offend anyone—they are simply focusing on goals and will do anything to accomplish them.

#10: Workplace bullies are nothing more than assertive managers or co-workers

Assertive managers lead with an "iron fist," and they make things happen. Their only goal is to get the job done. They might be loud once in a while, but they are fair and treat everyone equally. Assertiveness is about respecting other people's boundaries, listening, and considering other people's points of view without threatening them or dominating the conversation. Assertive managers might be frustrating to work with sometimes because they will stand their ground, but assertive managers are ultimately fair and respected by their peers and subordinates.

Bullies, on the other hand, are loud and offensive, and they belittle, torment, and manipulate. In other words, bullies are aggressive. Aggressive is different from assertive—aggressive people are not reasonable, do not have control over their anger, dominate conversations, and argue to win.

The bottom line is that assertive managers manage and bullies mismanage. Assertive co-workers try to get everyone on board to accomplish company objectives; bullying co-workers try to get their way by stomping on the rights and dignity of the people around them.

#11: Bullying is just media hype

We hear this myth quite a bit, and nothing could be further from the truth.

> **Tough boss vs bullying boss**
>
> Tough Boss
> - Coaches performance using goals and rewards
> - Gives credit when it's due
> - Motivates employees to succeed with assertive communication
> - Tells employees why they won't be included on a project anymore
>
> Bullying Boss
> - Calls employees "stupid" when they aren't performing
> - Takes credit for others' work
> - "Motivates" with arbitrary and punitive punishment
> - Removes job tasks with no rhyme or reason

In fact, the research on workplace bullying is so profound and bullying is so widespread that countries throughout the world are having public discussions about workplace bullying and attempting to enact anti-bully laws. In Australia, both Queensland and Victoria have laws against workplace bullying, as do the provinces of Quebec, Ontario, and Saskatchewan, Canada. France and Sweden also have laws against bullying, and Ireland's Labour Relations Commission published a manual providing businesses with the tools they need to address bullying in the workplace in 2002, complete with information about writing a corporate policy.

In the United Kingdom, two large groups—the Andrea Adams Trust and Dignity at Work Now (DAWN)—established themselves to create awareness of bullying at work. Since then, with the help of several unions, The Dignity at Work Bill has been introduced, though has not yet passed into law (Vega & Comer, 2005). Targets may be able to take action under the Health and Safety at Work Act of 1974, but this requires severe damage be done in order to win, such as serious psychological breakdowns, or may require the filing of criminal charges.

In the United States, The Healthy Workplace Bill proposes legislation against workplace bullying and has advocates working hard to get it passed in several states, though they have been unsuccessful. This bill proposes that the bullying is intentional, which could be hard to prove. Like the United Kingdom, currently a target of workplace bullying could take legal action for intentional infliction of emotional distress or wrongful termination, but again, these can be hard to prove and hard to win.

However, in the United States pockets of laws have started to spring up. In Ventura County, CA, for example, county employees are prohibited from engaging in workplace bullying. The state of Nevada recently revamped their school-age bullying laws and charged school districts with taking action against student bullying. Their laws also cover adults. In other words, if you are an adult working in the school system in Nevada, you are covered by laws against bullying perpetrated by teachers, principals, administrators, and so forth. Hopefully we will continue to see more generalized laws pop up all around the nation.

#12: Bullying targets are protected under harassment and hostile work environment laws

Many human resources professionals mistakenly believe that bullying is already covered under existing law. This simply is not the case. The criteria for a "hostile work environment" is indeed that the target feels abused at work, and as a result performance suffers. Hostile work environment laws, however, only cover protected classes. That means that if the bully is an "equal opportunity bully," and does not bully because of the nine protected classes, including race, color, gender, religious beliefs, national origin, age, familial status, or disability, then the bullying is legal. The fact that bullying is legal is the reason most organizations do not have an anti-bully corporate policy.

#13: Bullying can be resolved with an anti-bully corporate policy

Some companies attempt to put an end to workplace bullying by creating anti-bully policies. We can create policies until we run out of ink, but unless they are in alignment with the organization's overall vision, and leadership supports them 100%, it will be like they don't exist at all. Corporate policies are only as good as management and employees' support for them.

Our experiences with targets, bullies, and the companies who have to deal with workplace bullying have highlighted the importance of changes in attitudes and behavior from the top down. Policies, procedures, investigations, and platitudes do not stop workplace bullying—but with support from top management, they can be a great first step. Additional steps include comprehensive investigations of complaints, well-designed education programs, specialized training and coaching, and in some cases even an overhaul of the organization's culture. But we will get to that later.

CHAPTER 2: AN IN-DEPTH LOOK AT WORKPLACE BULLYING

Six concepts central to bullying & Five levels of aggression

Workplace bullying is systematic aggressive communication, manipulation of work, and acts aimed at humiliating or degrading targets. Bullying creates an unhealthy power imbalance between the bully and targets, and bullying often results in psychological consequences for targets and co-workers, and in enormous monetary damage to an organization's bottom line.

In this chapter, we will address a variety of levels of aggression— not all aggression is bullying. But before we discuss each level of aggression in detail, let's explore some concepts central to the issue of workplace bullying.

#1: Bullying is recurring, perpetual, and ongoing

If a person yells at you once or twice, this is impolite or perhaps uncivil, but it's probably not going to affect you very much over the long run. Bullying occurs when aggressive behaviors occur regularly and consistently, with no signs of improvement. Many researchers hesitate to call something bullying unless the behaviors are happening several times a week for a period of six months. We think, however, that if the behavior is consistent and your co-worker or boss shows no sign of relenting, then bullying is happening. You don't have to wait six months before you can officially say, "I'm being bullied."

#2: Bullying escalates in frequency and level of aggression over time

Sometimes co-workers can be a little mean, but if the rudeness never escalates beyond that, or doesn't get worse or more frequent as time goes on, then that person is just ill-mannered. And while annoying, perhaps you can take comfort in the fact that they are simply socially inept, and not out to make your life miserable. Bullying, on the other hand, becomes more frequent and more aggressive as time goes on.

#3: Bullying causes psychological harm to targets and witnesses

Bullying can be really hurtful. But you already know this.

We want to highlight, however, that witnesses are also affected by the workplace bullying. Even if someone doesn't feel like they are targeted, observing bullying behaviors is harmful to their mental psyche. In addition, witnesses live in a state of fear that they will be targeted next.

#4: Bullying is about power

The first time a person becomes aggressive with you, if you do not immediately become assertive and stand up for your rights, that person will continue to bully you because you have, in essence, given the green light that you will "take it." From the start of this first incident, the aggressor has power. Over time, as the bullying continues, the relationship between the bully and target becomes one of an unfair and unhealthy power imbalance. The perpetrator understands that he or she has power over the target, and the target believes the perpetrator indeed has that power and is unable to stand up against it.

Incidentally, the power imbalance between bully and target need not be formal. Approximately 70% of bullies bully subordinates, but that means 30% of bullies are bullying their peers or superiors (Rayner, 1997). Interestingly, when people do bully "up," or bully their managers or superiors, the bullying behavior seems to be more aggressive than when bullying "down" or bullying a subordinate (Matthiesen & Einarsen, 2007).

#5: Bullying causes communication breakdown among employees and managers

When bullying is allowed to happen at work, both targets and witnesses are afraid. Everyone, whether bullied or not, fears the next outburst or act of aggression, and this creates a chain of undesired effects. Targets and witnesses will try to stay out of the way of the bully and might be afraid to ask for the information necessary to properly complete their job tasks. For example, if a target needs an answer to a question, and the bullying manager has the answer, the target will dread approaching that manager and will likely never obtain the answer to his or her question. This means that any employee fearing that manager is not getting the information he or she needs to do the job right.

In addition, as we describe below in our list of bullying behaviors, bullies often use communication as a way to gain power over an individual, or purposefully sabotage work. The bully might, for example, purposefully omit the target from staff meetings in order to keep the target out of the loop. If the target is not at the meeting, but holds information that can further the group's goals, the entire group suffers as a result of this bullying tactic.

When these elements are present, this results in hindering the organizations' ability to provide excellent products and services to their customers, follow safety protocols, maximize performance, and maintain competitiveness, to name a few of the problems bullying creates.

#6: Organizational goals cannot be met when there's a bully, and the bottom line suffers

Communication among employees and their managers is paramount to an organization's success. If team members can't communicate, they can't meet their individual goals, and the organization can't meet its goals either. It's simple: anytime an organization allows suppression of communication, abusive behaviors, and unhealthy relationships to foster, it sets itself up for failure. Goals are not met in a timely manner and the bottom line suffers.

What kinds of behaviors are considered bullying behaviors?

Bullying behaviors may be inconspicuous or blatant—although according to much of the research on the subject, most bullies prefer passive and indirect behaviors. This makes sense if they are to avoid getting caught red-handed for abuse at work.

After reviewing several different measures researchers have used in surveying targets of bullying, we consolidated and categorized the many different behaviors listed in those measures into three different "buckets": communication, humiliation, and manipulation. As you review the list, put a checkmark next to the behaviors that you have witnessed in your workplace.

BULLYING BEHAVIORS

Communication

- ☐ Insulting, offensive or belittling remarks
- ☐ Shouting, yelling, angry outbursts
- ☐ Intimidation through finger-pointing, invasion of personal space, shoving, or blocking the way
- ☐ Staring others down, giving aggressive facial expressions or dirty looks
- ☐ Threatening employment termination, demotions, or removal of bonuses
- ☐ Avoiding communication altogether (by not returning phone calls or responding to emails, for example)
- ☐ Persistently criticizing
- ☐ Frequently interrupting peers when they are speaking
- ☐ Leaving the work area when certain individuals enter
- ☐ Demanding to get his or her way, forcing others to accept his or her point of view
- ☐ Isolating others by not inviting them to social events, leaving them out, and attempting to get others to ignore and isolate them
- ☐ Rolling eyes or making snide comments when peers talk or share ideas, consistently ignoring peer ideas and comments all together

Humiliation

- ☐ Humiliating or ridiculing co-workers in front of other people; excessive teasing
- ☐ Starting or spreading gossip and rumors
- ☐ Hinting to peers that they should quit, nobody likes them, or the boss thinks they are incompetent
- ☐ Consistently reminding others of mistakes they made in the past, not letting mistakes go, or making a bigger deal out of a mistake than it really is
- ☐ Playing harsh practical jokes
- ☐ Attacking the integrity of peers or claiming they are unethical
- ☐ Talking badly to management about others to make themselves look good or to get the other person in trouble or fired

☐ Discrediting a person professionally by attempting to make them feel worthless, or feel like others do not value their contribution

☐ Making fun of targets within earshot, so the target knows he or she is being ridiculed

Manipulation

☐ Withholding information co-workers need to do their jobs well, including excluding peers from memos, meetings, and other types of information or functions

☐ Removing responsibilities or important job tasks in order to threaten job security or humiliate targets

☐ Ordering subordinates to do work below their level of competence in order to humiliate them or hurt their production

☐ Ordering subordinates to do work above their level of competence to be sure they cannot complete the task and will appear incompetent

☐ Assigning work that is impossible to do, not providing accurate or complete instructions, or giving impossible deadlines

☐ Uber-excessive and unnecessary micromanagement

☐ Not allowing subordinates to take sick leaves, holidays, days off, or vacations

☐ Failing to give credit for a job well done or taking credit for other people's work

☐ Preventing access to opportunities such as a promotion or raise by telling others the candidate is not qualified or by claiming poor performance on an employee evaluation

☐ Frequently changing tasks to thwart performance or prevent completion of responsibilities

☐ Punitive and arbitrary punishment (e.g., writing an employee up for being one minute late) or inconsistent punishment

☐ Showing up late for meetings and other functions scheduled by specific co-workers to demonstrate they are unimportant

☐ Sabotaging others by damaging or stealing either their property, or property provided by the company that they need to do their work

In research that looked at which of these behaviors are the most severe, researchers Escartin, Rodriquez-Carballeira, Zapf, Porrua, and Martin-Pena (2009) found that the highest severity of bullying that caused the most psychological damage to targets were behaviors such as offensive actions and expressions that were specifically geared toward injuring and sneering at a co-worker's feelings. From the list above, these behaviors might include persistent criticism, insulting and offensive remarks, making snide comments about intelligence level or inability to perform work, and excessive teasing.

In the same study, manipulation of work and discrediting someone professionally were considered of middle severity by targets. These behaviors might include withholding information needed to do the job well, removing responsibilities to threaten job security, assigning work that is well beyond the target's competence, and taking credit for others' work.

Finally, for participants in this study, isolation was considered of lowest severity—not being invited to social events, feeling left out, and attempts from the bully to get others to ignore them affected participants the least.

In a nationwide study in Britain sponsored by the British Occupational Health Research Foundation (BOHRF) and conducted by the infamous workplace bullying researchers Hoel and Cooper (2000), participants were asked what bullying behaviors they were exposed to the most. The results indicated:

- 54% were ignored when giving their opinion
- 50% believed information had been withheld that affected their performance
- 46% were given unmanageable workloads
- 38% were given tasks with impossible deadlines

- 36% were ordered to do work below their level of competence
- 35% were ignored or faced hostility when they approached the bully
- 34% were ridiculed in connection with work
- 31% were the victims of gossip

In a study conducted by the Workplace Bullying Institute and Zogby International in 2007, survey respondents were asked to select any of the most common bullying behaviors they experienced. Behaviors were grouped together in categories, and the results showed that:

- 53% experienced verbal abuse, including shouting, name calling, malicious sarcasm, and threats to safety
- 53% experienced aggressive threats, intimidation, hostile actions, and inappropriately cruel conduct
- 47% felt the bully abused their authority by giving undeserved evaluations, denying promotions, taking credit for others' work, and giving unsafe assignments
- 45% indicated the bully had sabotaged or undermined them
- 30% felt the bully had destroyed their workplace relationships with co-workers, bosses, and even customers

When are these behaviors considered bullying?

Although a list of bullying behaviors can be useful in understanding what is happening to you at work, and describing your situation to friends, family, and managers, it is important to recognize that there are different levels of workplace bullying. Bullying can happen for many different reasons and in a vast variety of situations and contexts. When bullying occurs, it can happen on a spectrum of severity from incivility all the way up to violence.

As highlighted in Figure 2.1 below, there are five levels of workplace aggression. They are:

1. Incivility
2. Emotional Bullying
3. Predatory Bullying
4. Mobbing
5. Violence

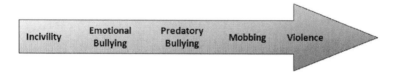

Figure 2.1. The Aggression Spectrum

#1: Incivility

Incivility and disrespect at work is unpleasant. It can be hurtful, frustrating, and uncomfortable, but it is not necessarily bullying. Incivility refers to the occasional rude comment during a staff meeting, loud outburst by a stressed out boss, showing up late to an appointment, or interrupting a colleague while he or she is talking. Although incivility can also have devastating effects on the workplace culture, such as increasing stress and reducing employee morale, these occasional stabs at your ego do not cause the same types of psychological trauma as workplace bullying.

People who are disrespectful may or may not realize when they are being rude. If your disrespectful co-workers are already aware of their behavior, then they might either apologize or just hope you will let it go, believing it's "no big deal." If your co-workers are not aware that their behavior is so hurtful, they may simply be lacking a little empathy, politeness, or effective communication skills.

You have two choices when it comes to a person who occasionally makes a rude comment—let it go and just know they aren't purposefully trying to hurt you, or say something to them about it. If you decide to speak up you may find they are shocked to hear that others find their behavior so upsetting and may try to change for the better... or they will become defensive. We cannot guarantee a positive outcome, but if you don't try to talk to them, the outcome will always be negative. Remember that if you do speak up, do it calmly and keep your professionalism.

#2: Emotional Bullying

Emotional bullying is the first level of true workplace bullying behaviors. Emotional bullying refers to the fact that some people are frustrated, stressed out, angry, having personal problems at home, or simply upset about something, and they respond by lashing out and bullying others. An emotional bully likely has no idea how awful he or she is treating others, and is not abusing others on purpose. In this case, bullying is simply an emotional outlet, and likely includes behaviors such as yelling at co-workers or subordinates, uber-excessive and unnecessary micromanagement, not allowing subordinates to take sick leaves or vacations, taking credit for other people's ideas to make themselves look good, or publicly criticizing co-workers.

Rocket science

Carol worked for a corporate attorney. The attorney was usually pretty nice, but he wasn't very good at giving specific directions. When people didn't do what he wanted exactly the way he wanted it, he got frustrated. Everyone dreaded his favorite condescending remark, "It doesn't take a rocket scientist," always delivered in an arrogant tone.

The attorney had extremely high turnover in receptionists and secretaries, until one day when Carol decided she'd had enough. The attorney was scolding her for something, and just as he started to say, "It doesn't..." she interrupted him and said, "We are all very intelligent people, but when you don't give very good directions, we can't do things the way you want them done. We're not rocket scientists, and we're not mind-readers."

The attorney was surprised, and then he asked, "Does it come across as rude when I say that?" Carol proceeded to advise the attorney that he'd actually lost many great employees because of this "rocket scientist" comment and lack of understanding in his own inability to give clear directions. The attorney was shocked that he had been perceived so awfully by others, and asked Carol to let him know whenever she felt like he was being rude to her. He also made a point of telling the rest of his employees that they had the same right. This attorney was not a bully; he was just disrespectful sometimes.

Emotional bullying can be compared to the typical Halloween cat with dilated pupils, arched back, hair standing up, poofed out tail, ears pointed straight up, and mouth open to display its fangs. A cat with this aggressive stance is simply responding to something in the environment, and is attempting to maintain its own safety by appearing larger and scarier than it really is (McEllistrem, 2004). Like in the cat, this kind of aggression is provoked by strong emotions that result in aggressive behaviors, dependent upon the environment and an individuals' repertoire of communication and behavior tactics. This reaction is simply in defense to a provocation, and bullying occurs because these people are lacking the appropriate communication skills they need to respond in a healthy and civilized manner.

#3: Predatory Bullying

Predatory bullying can be compared to the cat who becomes quiet, lowers itself to the ground, and inconspicuously tiptoes towards its prey until close enough to make a swift attack. This kind of bullying is deliberate, malicious, intentional, and a means to a desired end goal. These end goals might include "taking down" the people who threaten them by being intelligent or high producers, gaining power over others, or taking control over an environment that feels otherwise uneasy and out of control.

Gaining power over others is important to predatory bullies because they feel powerless for a variety of reasons. In many cases, predatory bullies are managers abusing or undermining subordinates because they are threatened by how good the subordinate's work quality is, or because their own work is of poor quality and they fear they will be discovered. In other cases, the bully feels power slipping through his or her fingers because the environment is changing—whether through the on-boarding of new and innovative employees with fresh ideas, looming layoffs, a change in organizational culture, or the witnessing of a boss' sincere respect for a counterpart in a different department.

Predatory bullies are perhaps the most damaging and hard to stop because they are intentionally hurting other people without regard for their feelings or the outcome of the bullying. Most of these predators do not have empathy for others, and thus they do not feel regret for the way they've acted; in fact, they might even feel joy when they see they've caused you pain. Predatory bullies choose their targets carefully, and their attacks are planned out meticulously.

As another major researcher in the field of workplace bullying (Einarsen, 1999) put it, this kind of bullying is initiated by a work-related conflict and is about "total destruction of the opponent" and overpowering the adversary. Ultimately, obtaining power over the target is the desired goal.

#4: Mobbing

Mobbing is a different kind of bullying—it is about a group of people who single out one person because that person is different in some way. Mobbing will occur most often when an outsider joins a group. For example, when a woman joins an otherwise all male group, such as the police force, firefighting, construction, or working the docks, or when a person of one race joins a group of people who are all of the same race. The point of mobbing behavior is to ostracize and ultimately remove the odd-person from the group; therefore, mobbers often do things to point out that the target is different, and attempt to prove this target

GI Jane and the Navy Seals

One clear example of mobbing is in the movie *GI Jane*, with actress Demi Moore playing the rouge Navy Seal hopeful, Jordan O'Neill. In the movie, Jordan enrolls in Navy Seal training—and because she is a woman, her fellow Seal trainees and instructors expect her to fail. In fact they do everything in their power to see that she does. Most of the movie focuses on Jordan's experiences being mobbed by fellow trainees and instructors. Despite psychological and physical abuse and even almost being raped, Jordan beats all odds by overcoming the brutal ridicule and proudly graduates.

cannot make it in "their" world. If they abuse the person long enough, then they can say that the target was a wimp and didn't belong there in the first place without taking responsibility for their own actions.

Mobbing includes such behaviors as hazing, writing offensive jokes on the target's locker, leaving inappropriate pictures aimed at the outsider hanging around the work area, calling the target rude names, yelling at the target for mistakes—real or fabricated—in front of the whole group, becoming openly angry when they are assigned to work with the target, or complaining regularly about the target's inability to perform.

#5: Violence

Some bullying behaviors escalate to threats of violence or violent behaviors. People who are bullying because they are predatory, and groups of people engaging in mobbing, are the most likely to escalate to this point. While violence at work is out of the scope of this book, for your safety we did want to touch on it briefly because it is the final stage in the aggression continuum, and because we wanted to warn you that bullying—when not dealt with properly—has the potential of escalating into violence.

As we have outlined in Figure 2.2. below, violent behavior is most likely to arise when the following four factors come together: attitudes, stress, setting, and a lack of communication skills.

Attitude

The way we view the world plays a huge part in how we respond to the diverse situations in which we find ourselves. Violent-prone individuals subscribe to a world-view of blame and lack of responsibility for their own actions, so in stressful or frustrating situations they see the external world as the reason for their problems. This leaves them feeling like they have no control, further escalating their frustration.

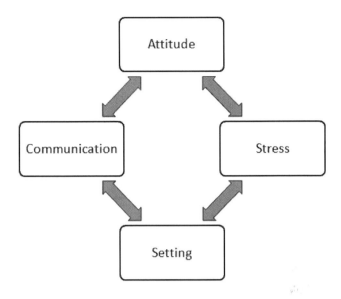

Figure 2.2. The four factors contributing to violent behavior at work

When someone else is to blame for a negative situation, how can a person take control and make the sitation better? For some the answer is to lash out verbally or even commit an act of violence. People who take responsibility for their own actions and believe their life is a product of their own choices, on the other hand, are much less frustrated with the world when something negative happens because they have control over their actions and believe they can change negative situations into positive ones. Rather than seeing no way out and resorting to violence, these individuals will find ways to improve the situation for which they believe they are responsible.

Stress

Escalated frustration in any of life's facets can make all of us a little irritable and even aggressive. Feeling stressed about workload, the work environment, home life, or a financial situation can easily bleed into other parts of our lives. Money problems at home, for example, can cause an individual's patience to wear thin and result in becoming aggressive with co-workers, even though the money problems and co-workers are not related.

According to The American Institute of Stress, the physical and psychological effects of stress are numerous and include headaches, tremors, overreaction to petty annoyances, insomnia, nightmares, feelings of worthlessness, obsessive behavior, anti-social behavior and withdrawal, fatigue, feeling overwhelmed, and a rather long list of other problems. Because violent-prone individuals passionately blame others for their stress, they are struck by an overwhelming sense of desperation and powerlessness. For them, violence is a way to gain back power and deal with the stress.

Setting

In the book, *The Violent-Prone Workplace: A New Approach to Dealing with Hostile, Threatening, and Uncivil Behavior*, authors Denenberg and Braverman point to several environmental sources of job-related pressures that increase the likelihood an individual will suffer a breakdown, including competition, loss of autonomy, increased surveillance, and changing demographics.

According to the authors, ever-changing technology; the global market; outsourcing of jobs; increased demand for efficiency and high production with less resources; long working hours with little time for vacations or time off; threats of mergers, downsizing, rightsizing and buy-outs; fast-moving changes in the way an organization functions; and ongoing change in the way business is done is enough to make anybody's head spin. All of this points to one thing: an increase in the struggle to stay competitive. For a person who blames others and doesn't handle stress well, working in an organization where these stressors are prominent and competition is fierce can be too much to handle.

Further, the United States is made up of thousands of races, nationalities, ethnicities, skin-colors, body shapes and sizes, socioeconomic classes, languages, religions, sexual orientations, and disabilities, with no sign of the population's continued metamorphosis letting up. In an organization that was once predominantly one "type" of group, these changes can lead to misunderstandings, lack of respect, and violence.

Ultimately, there is a difference between an organization that is dysfunctional and prone to incivility, bullying, and violence, and an organization that focuses on collaboration, civility, healthy relationships, safety, and violence-prevention. Managers and leaders are responsible for fostering this sort of environment, eradicating bullying immediately upon discovering it, and preventing violence.

Lacking communication skills

Violence is also the result of an inability to express oneself successfully. When a person feels like they cannot get their point across, or they are not being understood, they become frustrated and may lash out or resort to violence in order to gain control of the situation.

Because of this, organizations world-wide invest billions of dollars in communication and conflict management skill training. Afterall, effective communication skills are the foundation of productive teams and safe work environments. This is evident in hiring and firing practices—employees are often hired for technical skills but fired for lacking communication skills.

Spotting violent behaviors before they happen

Nearly two million American workers are victims of violence at work each year, according to the Occupational Safety & Health Administration (OSHA) here in the United States. Therefore we thought it worthwhile to offer a list of behaviors that signal a person is under extreme stress and may become violent, and a list of behaviors that you should watch out for during an interaction with an aggressive person at work (Canadian Centre for Occupational Health and Safety; OSHA; University of California, San Francisco).

While it is not always possible to predict with absolute certainty when someone will become violent, the behaviors in our lists below may provide some indication. Always take the behaviors in context – look for multiple signs, and watch for signs of escalation.

A person may become violent if they:
- Display outbursts of rage and anger, temper tantrums, crying or sulking
- Cooperate poorly with others and blame others for their problems or mistakes
- Display sudden changes in work patterns such as tardiness or absenteeism, changing work product levels, or making an increased number of mistakes
- Demonstrate extreme or bizarre behavior, or deep depression
- Abuse alcohol or drugs
- Have had a recent loss
- Are disgruntled more than usual about work, complain about work constantly, or talk about the same problems without taking steps to resolve them
- Are fixated on perceived injustices and unfair treatment
- Engage in behavior meant to sabotage

- Have a history of violent behavior
- Show an obsession with weapons; discuss weapons excessively at work, carry a concealed weapon, or flash a weapon
- Make either direct or implied verbal threats of harm
- Have an obsessive involvement with the job, with no apparent outside interests
- Are a loner who has little involvement with co-workers
- Are fascinated with recent incidents of workplace violence and openly approve of the use of violence
- Show an escalating propensity to push the limits of normal conduct, disregarding the safety of co-workers
- Are highly suspicious or paranoid, and believe that the whole world is against him or her
- Handle criticism poorly, or overreact to criticism, and show a clear disrespect for authority
- Refuse to acknowledge job performance issues when problems are brought to their attention
- Hold grudges and often verbalize a hope for something to happen to the person against whom they have a grudge
- Express extreme desperation over recent family, financial, or personal problems
- Make faulty decisions and/or show an inability to focus

Communication that signals a person may immediately become violent include:

- Becoming white or red-faced
- Pacing or other restless, repetitive movements; inability to sit down; appearing anxious
- Trembling or shaking, tense muscles
- Clenched teeth and tense lips
- Exaggerated or violent gestures
- Loud chanting or talking; yelling

- Scowling, sneering or using abusive language; making verbal threats
- Leaning into, or violating, personal space
- Shallow and rapid breathing
- Never ceasing eye contact; harshly glaring, never looking away
- Appearing as though they are ready to swing, whether through arms held back slightly or a shifting of weight to the back leg like a fighter
- Arms crossed on the chest, closed fists; hands held tightly against the chest (that could indicate they are holding a weapon)

Do not ignore or downplay direct or indirect threats from any person. They can escalate into serious incidents.

We reiterate that this section about violence is in no way comprehensive, and is only meant to offer some introductory information about violence at work. If you believe your safety is being threatened, report it to management immediately.

On a final note, the bully isn't the only person who may become violent. When a target of bullying is unhappy, he or she might also become violent and turn on the bully. If you are experiencing thoughts of violence, remember that your job and unhappiness is not worth the bully's life or your time in jail. If violence is starting to feel like the only answer, it is time to get a new job, period.

CHAPTER 3: WHY THERE ARE BULLIES

Eleven reasons people bully at work

We have just provided a little insight as to the different levels of bullying behaviors one might experience at work. As you may have realized, the world's population is not divided into two: people who bully and people who do not. At one time or another, we all display negative behaviors that can range from subtle acts of incivility to losing our temper or even a physical altercation. Of course, we like to think most of us only occasionally display acts of incivility—we have all spread a rumor, ignored someone, or barked in annoyance at a family member, customer or co-worker. But unlike us, bullies consistently display behaviors that go way beyond incivility. As we discussed in the previous chapter, bullies can be manipulative, seek opportunities to humiliate targets, and are overtly aggressive and intimidating on a regular basis.

You should also be aware that context makes a huge difference in how a person behaves. Someone who is a target of bullying at work might actually be considered a bully by other co-workers or subordinates. In other words, you can be a target and a bully all at the same time.

In any case, according to the scientific research on bullying at work, as well as our own experiences, there are a myriad of reasons a person might exhibit bullying behaviors with co-workers, peers, managers, or subordinates. We have provided a list of the most common ones below. A person exhibiting bullying behaviors may be doing so because of all of the reasons listed, or any combination thereof.

#1: Feelings of insecurity

Most of us walk around with some type of insecurity. Some are terribly threatened by other people, challenges, new assignments, and new hurdles, while others are afraid of meeting people, public speaking, or making sales calls. When we are feeling insecure, we feel like everyone can see it, and we feel uncomfortable and powerless. Some people attempt to regain that power, and become more comfortable with their situation, by becoming aggressive.

People who suffer from constant insecurities might feel that way because they are:

- Threatened when their competency or decision making is challenged by others
- Afraid that their lack of skill will make them look foolish, and they will be viewed as a fraud
- Not comfortable with criticism or challenges
- Not aware that cooperation gets more stuff accomplished than conflict
- Untrusting of the team or specific members of the team
- Living what they would consider a "hard life" and are frustrated or embarrassed because of it, or act tough in order to show pride in their "roots"
- Constantly worried they cannot meet their deadlines
- Dependent upon the work of others but are not comfortable with that
- Defensive and treat every challenge as a life or death situation
- Unable or unwilling to empathize
- Always operate in survival mode, working on putting out the latest "major fire"
- Feeling excluded, or left out of the "in-crowd," so respond by lashing out at them.

The bullying supervisor

In the HR department of a company with 18,000 employees, the team of people who worked on employee benefits had worked together for some time. Tenure ranged from eight years all the way up to twenty-two years. The group of women working in the department was a tight-knit one—they even had regular outside events including Saturday family BBQ's and birthday parties. When the new supervisor got there, it all changed.

A supervisor had retired, so a new one was hired in to manage this bunch of women who were such close friends. One by one, the new supervisor tortured them. Essentially, she chose one employee and harassed, picked on, and verbally abused her until she couldn't take it anymore and quit. Immediately, the supervisor then targeted someone else, and when she quit, the supervisor chose someone else, and so forth.

Not one of the eight women who worked there at the start of this supervisor's reign is there anymore. Still, the women are shocked and confused. How could management ignore that they'd all been there for so long, right up until the new supervisor was hired? Wasn't it obvious there was something wrong with the way the supervisor managed? Clearly, the new supervisor was threatened by how close the women were, and sought to destroy their relationships. Now she's got a new team of people, and control over their relationships.

#2: Lacking resourcefulness

Some people are really great at finding what they need to make a project a success, can find the resources they need to make something happen, or seem to just "get it" and are great at figuring things out even when they don't know anything about them. These kinds of people take failures as learning opportunities and are always seeking new information and new understanding of the world around them.

But for some, resourcefulness is not a strength and knowledge and resources don't seem to come so easily. Unfortunately, lack of knowledge and resources can create a breeding ground for bullying behaviors because these individuals:

- Lack competence and are limited by their inability to get the proper resources that would support them in completing their tasks, and often feel they are in over their heads
- Don't know how to do their work and attempt to make up for it with aggression
- As a result of their attitude, don't have the team-support, finances, or necessary resources to complete their tasks and are frustrated by it
- Draw conclusions based on very little factual information, and then make decisions based on incomplete data, which results in frustration with the decision and the poor outcome
- Choose to attack (or counterattack, in their mind) when confronted with a challenge or results of a poor decision, instead of calmly discussing solutions to the problem at hand.

#3: Feeling all-powerful or powerless

As we mentioned in the previous chapter, power is central to the concept of workplace bullying. During the first incident of aggression towards you, if you do not stand up for yourself and respond immediately in an assertive manner, the power struggle begins. Over time, as the bullying continues and escalates, you and this individual begin to understand your roles in the relationship you've developed to be one of a powerful (bully) and a powerless (you). These positions are reinforced every time you communicate or interact, making you an active participant in creating and maintaining this power imbalance. Later in this book, we will provide information to end this disparity.

Bullies have an interesting relationship with power—they become aggressive when they feel like they have a lot of it, and they become aggressive when they feel like they have none of it. The only time they don't bully is when they are happy with the amount of power they have.

Researcher Blake Ashforth, who refers to bullying as "petty tyranny," points out that some people are overbearing and domineering, insistent upon their own rules and their own way, and assert the rights their organizational status affords them. These people believe their peers are lazy and irresponsible, so they often become aggressive to get their own needs met (1994). Ashforth also points out that some individuals who have power, such as managers, will capitalize on the power they have because it boosts their self-esteem or because they believe that leadership means creating a power distance between themselves and their "minions." These people exploit their authority and take advantage of their position. Unfortunately, these people also have corporate tools at their fingertips to bully with, such as employee evaluations, disciplinary procedures, and an HR department who will likely take their side should something go awry.

Others, without any power, such as a clerk who can't seem to get ahead, will create an environment where they do have power to make themselves feel better, and they do so by instilling fear in those around them.

Whether they are bullying because they believe they have a lot of power, or bullying because they believe they have no power, these individuals:

- Micromanage in order to assert dominance and because they honestly believe the people they work with can't be trusted to do their work right
- Put people down in order to make themselves feel good
- Attempt to control the workflow and work product of the people around them, by withholding information for a few days before releasing it, for example
- Do not handle stress very well because it leaves them feeling like they have no control
- Become angry when decisions are made without their input
- Expect people to value their opinion and see their way as the right way, and therefore don't take the time to offer a professional, persuasive argument when presenting their ideas
- Want things done a certain way simply because they said so
- Use rules (e.g., corporate policies, laws, state codes) to back up their stance on a position, follow those rules *exactly* as they were written without room for interpretation, and target people perceived as rule-violators.

#4: Lacking effective communication skills

Effective communicators have the ability to empathize, listen without judgment, and reach outside of themselves to really make an effort to understand the person to whom they are talking. Clearly, bullies do not have these types of skills. There is a wealth of research that supports the notion that if you cannot communicate very well, you will resort to aggression and even violence, because you're frustrated with the fact that you can't get your point across or that people don't seem to understand you.

It is certainly an art to be able to deal with conflict in a healthy way. Most people think conflict or arguments are about getting the other person to see their point of view and ultimately to win. What they are forgetting is that the person they are arguing with probably also wants their point of view to be heard, and likely also wants to win. In order for conflict to be resolved, at least one of the parties has to relinquish the desire to win at all costs, and see a value in listening to the other person. As leadership expert, Steven Covey, so wisely said, "Seek first to understand, then to be understood." By doing that, it is easier to get to a compromise and a solution.

Obviously, people who resort to bullying don't "seek first to understand." Instead, aggressive people might be:

- Lacking the ability to successfully and calmly persuade others to get what they want, so they use aggression instead
- Unable to articulate their point of view well and in a manner that others can understand
- Unable to stay rational and calm during disagreements
- Lacking in self-control
- Prone to outbursts of anger because they don't understand the value of withholding them
- Unaware that their communication style is hurtful
- Lacking in the ability to listen carefully to another person's point of view without judgment
- Communicating in a nasty way because they learned that communication style from someone else, such as a parent, older sibling, or tenured co-worker

- Continuing to bully because they learned that it works for them—they feel powerful and a sense of accomplishment when pushing people around, and have found that many people usually give in
- Convinced that negative or aggressive messages are an appropriate way to manage conflict
- Argumentative because they like to be that way—winning arguments or proving they are right feels good to them, even at the cost of hurting others.

#5: Lacking leadership skills

Some people are really good leaders naturally; it just comes to them effortlessly. They have a great personality, people adore them, and people flock to them because of their charisma and ability to get people motivated to be great and do great things. But not everyone is naturally a great leader, and because they don't know how to get people motivated, they resort to aggression. In many cases, people do not start bullying others until they have been given a management position.

Poor leaders might resort to aggression because they:
- Do not feel comfortable in a leadership position
- Never learned to effectively communicate goals and objectives like a true leader should
- Are disorganized and cannot focus or prioritize
- Are overwhelmed with deadlines and the diverse responsibilities management entails
- Like to keep employees "on their toes" by changing priorities
- Do not keep track, nor can they remember, what has been delegated

The manufacturing plant

A manufacturing plant in Northern California has been around for over thirty years, but strangely enough, they have never put a leadership training program into place. For years, the family oriented company has promoted from within, and a person hired in to work the line at eighteen could be a supervisor by twenty-five if they worked hard, followed the safety guidelines, and had a high level of production.

One college student was hired in to the engineering department as an intern. Showing potential immediately, he was hired and climbed "the ranks" quickly. Now a top-level manager, he has developed a sense that everyone around him is incompetent—after all, look how quickly he worked his way to the top!

Unfortunately, because he was promoted to leader so soon, he never received leadership training and has turned into someone everyone else brands as a bully.

As long as such behaviors are tolerated, the company is doomed to have a culture of fear and a feeling of oppression, which negatively affects productivity. While the president avoids taking steps to implement a leadership-development program, the company and its employees' success will never raise beyond mediocrity.

In fact, due to the bully's behavior and lack of collaboration, one maintenance manager reported that he once had to fix a machine while it was 420°. Now, due to verbal abuse and the resulting inability to communicate with him, an employee's safety was severely compromised.

If only the president would teach the manager how to be a leader…

- Enjoy making others feel afraid or insecure
- Like to micro-manage in order to feel powerful, or in charge of "something"
- Do not trust their employees and hence do not delegate; they believe they must do everything in order to be sure tasks are done right
- Have a personal bias against a subordinate and allow those feelings to show though
- Believe those they perceive as incompetent should be singled out and thrown out of the organization.

#6: Easily provoked or have a low tolerance for stressful situations

Workplace bullying is often associated with stressful environments. Researchers have found that when things are stressful at work, people become aggressive. Naturally, some people will handle stress better than others. People who don't handle stress very well, however, may start to exhibit bullying behaviors as they are struggling to deal with their internal issues generated by feeling stressed out. We've all been under strict deadlines or pushed to our limit at work, and many of us have likely become slightly more irritable than we normally are during those circumstances. But people who turn into bullies are so affected by stress that hostility becomes a way of life.

People with low tolerance for stress might become belligerent when:

- The work environment is competitive
- Another co-worker is promoted or chosen for a job assignment that they wanted
- They are frustrated by someone they perceive to be underperforming

- People around them appear to violate the policies and rules the organization has in place
- They are dissatisfied with a job or organization
- The organization downsizes, merges with another company, or makes other changes
- Job responsibilities are not clear, or job tasks are reorganized and shifted around
- Their work load is ever changing and therefore confusing
- Performance measures are not in place within the organization, leaving employees to guess when they are doing a good job
- They and their co-workers haven't received the proper training to do their jobs, so are left feeling confused about what to do and how to do it well.

#7: Their belief system supports bullying as acceptable behavior

Some people simply subscribe to a belief system that doesn't make sense to the rest of us. When identifying a course of action in any situation, people with what we might call a "moral distortion" will choose to be disrespectful and unprofessional to get what they want because they believe it works. Belief systems also extend to beliefs about other people. In one author's research, for example, she found that bullying behaviors are a result of believing others are incompetent (Mattice, 2007).

People with this corrupt belief system think:
- That leaders must be gruff and abrasive to be powerful
- That people perform better when they're intimidated
- That sensitivity and time spent being nice is a waste of time

- That some people are naturally less talented or reliable, and it's okay to yell at them
- That most people are lazy, underperforming, and try to avoid responsibilities
- Motivation by fear is better than motivation by positive reinforcement
- That they are always right
- That punishments are appropriate for anyone who challenges or defies them
- That change is bad for the team, unless the change is one that they came up with
- That they're too busy, important, or driven to be nice to others who aren't at their level or standards
- That they are simply better than everyone else, and attack anyone who seems to think otherwise
- It is okay to verbally attack others in order to blow off steam or get back at someone for doing something they didn't agree with
- That they have a passion for work and a commitment to the organization's success that no one else shares
- That arguing to win is appropriate, even if it means crushing the person with whom they are arguing.

#8: Personality disorder

When this subject came up as we were writing the book, we hesitated to even mention it. But we wanted to give you all of the information you need about bullying so you can successfully fight it, so we decided to at least touch upon this topic. We simply want you to understand that it is possible that bullying is a result of some personality disorder, such as being a psychopath or sociopath—but unless you are a psychiatrist or psychologist, please do not attempt to diagnose your co-workers. The media loves to paint bullies as psychopaths who have no control and are out for blood. But the fact is, researchers estimate that only about 5% of the population is psychopathic, which means most bullies are not psychopaths at all. As we are attempting to demonstrate with this chapter, many people bully simply because they do not have the communication skills or wherewithal to handle themselves in ways that are positive.

#9: Personality style clashes

Our personalities are an innate part of who we are. Conflict, bullying, and other such controversy may sometimes be the result of a lack in understanding of differences in personality styles and hence intolerance of behavioral and communication differences. Of course, there is one personality style—as you'll read in the description below—that has a natural tendency to be more assertive, and that "assertiveness" might be viewed as aggression or bullying by people with other personality styles. However, most of those negative behaviors are not personal but rather are a function of that individual's natural wiring. This isn't an excuse for anyone's bad behavior, by the way, just an explanation.

What we are talking about here is something called the DISC Behavioral Model, or DISC. The acronym DISC refers to four styles of personality: Dominance, Influence, Steadiness, and Conscientiousness. The DISC model does not suggest that we are all stuck in one behavioral style or another. It is designed to raise awareness of our tendencies and the tendencies of those around us; then use this knowledge to take control—or gain acceptance—of our weaknesses and limitations, while focusing on capitalizing on our strengths and developing more successful relationships.

The DISC theory was originally developed by psychologist William Moulton Marston in the late 1920s, and in the following decades his findings were further developed and researched by various scientists. Since then the DISC model has become very popular in business. As you read, take a peek at Figure 3.1 below to get a visual of where each style falls on two different continuums: orientation to work and orientation to people. See if you recognize your personality style and the styles of your co-workers. Keep in mind that most of us are a combination of one or more of these styles, but usually one of the styles is more dominant within us.

Dominance (D-Style – Fast Paced & Task Oriented)

D-style individuals are characterized by a fast work pace, fast rate of speech, strong desire to be in charge, and intense focus on accomplishing goals and completing tasks. On the job, they are the ones who lead by example while pushing everyone to perform. They leave little room for personal chit-chat or other activities not related to work-objectives. They know what they want, they go for it, and they expect those around them to do the same. D-style individuals are goal-oriented, process driven, and often turn out to become real achievers. D's try to avoid, whenever possible, routine work and environments where they are not given the freedom to be in charge of their own actions, and are not allowed to move at their own (fast) pace.

Influence (I-Style – Fast Paced & People Oriented)

High I-style individuals are characterized by fast pace—both in actions and speech—and a love of socializing. I-style individuals are easily recognized by their high energy levels, enthusiasm, and openness to interaction with others at any moment of the day. They tend to smile when interacting with others and are seemingly always ready to share a joke or humorous story. They will also listen to the stories of others, even though listening is not their main strength and they'd rather talk than listen. They come across as friendly, enthusiastic, and passionate. At times they can be perceived as fake (too much smiling and enthusiasm) and tiring (too much talking). I-style individuals dislike environments where they are not given the freedom to interact with others, have to perform routine and detail-oriented activities, or are not given a chance for quick and regular recognition.

Steadiness (S-Style – Moderate Paced & People Oriented)

High S-style individuals are characterized by moderate pace—both in speech rate and physical movement—and by a strong desire to support others. S-style individuals enjoy being around people, and due to their thoughtful and caring nature, are great listeners and come across as friendly and warm. S-style people are calm, amiable, and supportive. They are perceived by many to be kind, and most of us enjoy having them around.

S-style individuals will often try to avoid fast-paced environments with unpredictable work schedules and will stay away, as much as possible, from any situations where they would have to put up with regular conflict or other stress. As the name of their personality style suggests, they like to work in environments where there's relative security and where they can work steadily at their routine tasks.

Conscientiousness (C-Style – Moderate Paced & Task Oriented)

High C-style individuals are characterized by moderate pace and cautiousness, and are highly task oriented. C-style individuals enjoy working individually or with a small group of other C-style individuals. They like getting deeply involved in performing tasks and do not like to be interrupted while working. They tend to be very particular about doing an excellent job and are very organized.

87

Due to their natural tendency to be analytical, C-style individuals are great in any area where accuracy and precision is needed. To the other three styles, C-style individuals can at times come across as distant, perfectionist, and overly nit-picky. C-style individuals will try to avoid fast-paced environments where they'd have to make quick decisions, spend most of their time on social niceties, and would have no time to carefully plan their days.

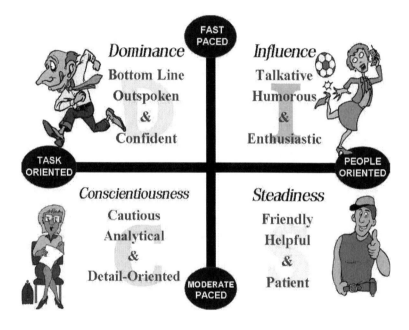

Figure 3.1. The DISC Model
(Source: Communication Skills Magic - reprinted with permission of the author)

As you can see in the graphic, every adjacent style has something in common: D's and I's are fast paced; I's and S's are people oriented; S's and C's are moderate paced; and C's and D's are task oriented. However, the opposing styles—C and I, and S and D—have no common traits, which naturally set these opposing styles up for conflict and perhaps even bullying if the environment is right. Often when working with someone of an opposing style, you don't even know why there's a tension in the air, you just feel that the other person doesn't like you and you don't really like them.

It is said that perception is everything, and that's definitely true when we speak about differences in personality styles. For example, when D and S-style individuals work as part of the same team, both can get annoyed at the other's way of doing things. The D-style individual can get frustrated by the S-style's slower pace and hesitant nature, as the S-style naturally takes time to think things through before engaging in an activity. This is unlike the D-style, who often makes quick decisions and acts on those decisions immediately. The S-style is also likely to become aggravated by the D-style's "frantic" pace, pushy nature, and bossy and ostensibly cold communication style.

It is not uncommon that the D-style teammate will lose his temper and raise his voice to try to "motivate" the S-style to "get with the program"; while the S-style might purposefully slow down and even resist performing certain tasks out of rebellion against the pushy and loud D-style. Both might view the other as a bully and a pain in the...well, a pain to work with. The negative behaviors of the two sides just do not balance out—the D-style's yelling and attempts to intimidate the S-style with blunt and often cruel comments are far more viewed as bullying behaviors than the S-style's slower pace or resistance to work with a pushy coworker. This is not to say that S-style individuals are saints; simply that their aggression or bullying might come in much subtler forms than the D-style's negative behaviors.

I and C-styles naturally clash in the workplace as well. I-style individuals are sociable, humorous, and talkative individuals who can often be terribly annoyed by the C-style's tendency to expect perfection in everything, high focus on the tasks they work on, serious demeanor, and obsession with following the rules. I-styles often don't mind bending some rules and at times are not even aware of them, while C-styles know all of the rules and follow them to the letter. On the other hand, the C-style, who is committed to doing an excellent job, is annoyed by the I-style's constant chit-chat and lack of focus.

All of these differences and annoyances can escalate in some individuals to conflict, acts of incivility, or even bullying. Bullying triggered as result of personality style clashes often develops from a lack of understanding of the diverse nature of human behavior and extreme frustration of not having one's own expectations met.

Bullying and the four personality styles

Each of the personality styles may bully in their own way. Below is a list of bullying behaviors each style might exhibit.

D Style – May use aggressiveness, pushiness, loud voice or yelling, bluntness, and profanities.

I Style – May use sarcasm, cruel jokes, gossip, and fabricated or blown-out-of-proportion condescending stories.

S Style – May use subtle bullying behaviors, such as withholding information, spreading rumors, slowing down work, or refusing to do tasks outside of their job description.

C Style – May withhold critical information, ask others to perform tasks beyond their competence level, refuse communication beyond the necessary minimum, use stern facial expressions, and criticize the work of others.

#10: People who witness the behavior do not stand up to the bully

Bystanders, as researchers call them, are the group with the most power to stop bullying, yet they are notorious for not saying anything when they see it happening. This is interesting because in a work team of seven people, for example, where one person is targeting another, it seems reasonable to assume that the other five people in the team would speak out on behalf of the target. Five people are certainly "stronger" than one bullying co-worker. But, this isn't usually what happens.

Unfortunately, bystanders, or witnesses to the abuse, are concerned about their own well-being and are afraid of being targeted next if they do stand up to a bullying co-worker. They just want to stay safe by staying out of it. For the same reason, they are also not willing to help you report the behavior to managers.

Researchers have repeatedly found that bystanders take a spectrum of positions in relation to the target and bully, as outlined in Figure 3.2 below. Why witnesses take a certain stance is not totally understood, although we are probably safe to assume it has something to do with their own personality, communication style, organizational rank, and pre-existing friendships.

Bully's assistant: These individuals often join in on the bullying. While their behavior isn't as severe as bullying, they may laugh at the bully's snide comments or help the bully sabotage your work.

Reinforcer: These individuals reinforce bullying behavior by not saying anything at all to the bully or to management. Reinforcers see what's happening and feel uneasy all of the time because they are in a state of fear for their own safety. Unlike the bully's assistant, who might participate in some of the bullying, reinforcers prefer to keep to themselves to avoid getting involved. Essentially, these individuals inactively support bullying by keeping their heads in the sand as a defense mechanism.

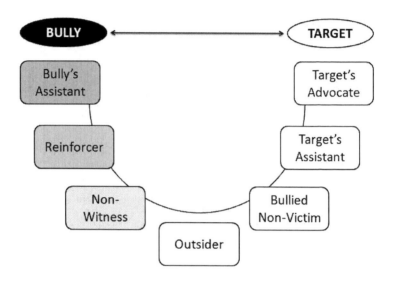

Figure 3.2. Bystander positions in relation to the bully and target

Non-witness: Non-witnesses are individuals who witness bullying behavior, but if asked whether bullying exists in their organization, their answer is "no." These individuals likely have a high tolerance for stress and aggression. This means that although they witness bullying behaviors regularly, to them it doesn't seem like bullying so they are not bothered by it. Perhaps they have always worked in aggressive workplaces so the bullying is nothing new, or they've come to believe aggression is a normal part of business. Either way, although by researcher's standards these individuals have witnessed bullying, they don't recognize it as such.

Outsider: These individuals simply do not see the bullying take place. Perhaps they are not very aware of their surroundings, the bullying goes on behind closed doors, or they do not associate with the bully or target and therefore do not witness exchanges between them. Outsiders are lucky enough to avoid bullying behaviors within their organization altogether…that's not to say that in time they may find themselves reporting to one.

Bullied "non-victim": This category is full of people who are bullied by researchers' standards, but do not identify themselves as a target of bullying for three separate reasons. First, they might think the bully is a jerk or an annoyance with a bad attitude, but have not allowed the bully to penetrate their psyche or upset them. Essentially, they are ultimately not bothered by these behaviors to the extent that a self-identified target might be. Second, much like the "non-witnesses," these individuals might believe that aggression is just the way it is or a normal course of business and therefore do not self-identify as a target of bullying. Third, "non-victims" might be in a position where the bully is unable to gain power over them so the bullying is irrelevant to them. For example, a co-worker in another department might be bullied by your own manager once in awhile, but won't see the bully as a threat the same way you do because they aren't frequently interacting with him or her, and therefore will not self-identify as a target.

Target's assistant: Some people witnessing bullying at work will take the side of the target. Hopefully you have found a support group in these people. These are people to whom you can turn in order to vent about your situation. Keep these people close; they are there to help you get through this. You may find, however, that they are not willing to come with you to talk to management or are unwilling to stand up for you in public. Remember that they are cautious to get involved publicly because they don't want to attract the attention of the bully.

Target's advocate: Unfortunately, there aren't too many of these people out there because of the dangers associated with this position. Research has found, however, that when these people exist the bullying quickly ends. If one member of your support system is willing to stand up for you, then take them up on it. Ask them to speak out to the bully when you are mistreated and to accompany you to a formal grievance report with your manager.

The interesting part about all of this is that witnesses—even those witnesses who claim they are not bothered by the bullying—are indeed affected. People who are not bullied, but witness bullying regularly, experience many of the same feelings targets of bullying do. Witnesses are anxious, fearful, and upset. And, over time, these bystanders lose faith in management and their company, which affects their work productivity too.

#11: Your workplace has a bully-friendly work environment or culture

Much of the time, a person bullies simply because he or she can—the organization allows it. Organizational leaders might be bullies themselves, so that behavior is picked up by others and trickles down though the ranks, or leaders simply do not see a problem and hence never address it. In a highly competitive workplace, for example, such as sales, law, academia, and medicine, bullying behavior often thrives. Many people enter the field to help others, but as time goes by, opportunities for advancement shrink. If you have one hundred medical students, for example, perhaps you have ten paid internships. So people respond by using every competitive advantage they have, including bullying.

Some organizations reward technical skills or big earners without holding people accountable for treating others with respect. Unfortunately, sometimes the most valued employee is also the one who causes the most trouble. The organization thinks they have to choose expertise or big money earners over collaborative behavior. But technical expertise, money, and appropriate behavior are not mutually exclusive, with some training and management focus on helping this individual improve communication skills, the organization can have its cake and eat it too.

Other organizations have failures of supervision, or weak leadership when it comes to demonstrating appropriate and productive behaviors. If you work in an organization with weak or absent leaders where there is little accountability for behavior and performance, you have a breeding ground for bullying behavior. We may all appreciate it when no one is breathing down our neck, but it's easy to misbehave when no one's watching or holding people accountable for their actions. Further, some organizations just have leaders who are bullies, so others follow suit.

Does your organization foster a culture of workplace bullying?

Bullying behaviors often occur when the organization allows them to. If managers and leaders were to step in and address the behavior, for example, the bullying behaviors would STOP. Take this assessment to find out if your workplace fosters a culture of workplace bullying.

Circle yes or no for each of the following questions.

1.	Does your organization acknowledge or give awards for effective communication skills?	Yes	No
2.	Do company meetings start with an open forum, where people are allowed to openly share ideas, thoughts, questions, and concerns?	Yes	No
3.	Are bonuses and other rewards directly related to positive evaluations of communication and interpersonal skills?	Yes	No
4.	During training sessions, does your organization promote and emphasize a culture of respect and civility?	Yes	No
5.	Is your team generally collaborative, where everyone feels free to offer suggestions and information to make projects successful?	Yes	No
6.	Are yours and other employee evaluations focused on strengths and opportunities for growth?	Yes	No
7.	Do your managers encourage employees to think for themselves, and trust employees to make the right decisions?	Yes	No

8.	Does your organization provide training and other types of programs that focus on topics such as interpersonal skills, leadership, and teamwork?	Yes	No
9.	Have you or a coworker made a complaint to your manager that you were being treated disrespectfully, only to be dismissed?	Yes	No
10.	Is there unhealthy competition among staff?	Yes	No
11.	Is your organization going through stressful organizational changes without much communication from the top about what will happen?	Yes	No
12.	Does your organization strictly enforce and follow rules, policies, and guidelines in order to do *anything*?	Yes	No
13.	Do employees spend a lot of time complaining about "the way it is around here" or about management?	Yes	No
14.	Are you and your co-workers generally stressed out about short deadlines, impossible workloads, and other types of workplace stressors?	Yes	No
15.	Have you seen others yelled at, attacked, ridiculed, or made to look stupid without any intervention from management to get the behavior to stop?	Yes	No
16.	Is feedback from your manager usually focused on what you're doing wrong, instead of what you are doing right? Does this feedback lack suggestions for improvement?	Yes	No

Take a look at your answers. If you answered "no" to any of questions 1–8, or "yes" to any of questions 9–16, it is very possible your organization is allowing bullying to thrive.

Organizations that focus on respect, civility, collaboration, innovation, and positive internal relationships generally would not allow bullying people to behave that way. Organizations that have a highly competitive environment and leaders who do not step in when someone is being disrespectful probably have bullying. Organizations that focus only on what is being done wrong and how to fix it, and think about the bottom line more their most valuable asset—employees—foster a workplace where bullying is just a normal way of life.

Please note that this assessment cannot and should not replace a corporate culture assessment or communication audit completed by a trained consultant. This assessment is meant to help you gauge what part your management and workplace culture might play in the issue of workplace bullying, but only an experienced consultant can conduct a climate assessment to determine where and why bullying behaviors occur.

CHAPTER 4: WHY ME?

Eleven reasons you might be targeted

Before we explore potential reasons why anyone would choose to bully you, it is important to understand the following:

a) No one deserves to be bullied or abused in any way for ANY reason.
b) NOTHING justifies bullying or mistreatment of another person.
c) Bullying is UNACCEPTABLE, and if it's happening to you, do whatever it takes to stop it and stay mentally and physically healthy.

Bullying is an interaction between two people. That means, even though you don't deserve to be abused at work, at times there's something about you, your behavior, or your position that gets your co-worker worked up or arouses a desire to turn on you. Understanding this can give you the power to stop the unwanted behaviors. We are not believers in the victim-mentality, or claiming there's nothing you could've done differently. Communication is a transaction between two people, and telling you that you are a completely innocent bystander in the transaction would be flat out propaganda. We must reiterate, we are NOT blaming you or saying you deserved to be treated poorly – but we are saying that if you look at your role you can change it from target to something more powerful. Without a full analysis of the bullying dynamic, true growth cannot take place.

We know this is hard to hear, and you're probably thinking that you're just a hard worker—someone who just wants to get the job done. What could you possibly have done to provoke abuse from another person?

We hesitated to write this chapter because we would never want you to feel responsible for what's happening to you or that you are at fault. But if we didn't include this chapter in the book, we would be doing you a disservice. The only way you can change your situation is by recognizing it for what it is. As you read the points below, you'll find that some are focused on you, some are focused on the bully, and some are focused on the organization.

This chapter is a distillation of perspectives that come from our work with people who have been bullied, our communication skills coaching work with people who are bullies, from our consulting work with organizations who have called upon us to assist in eradicating bullying, and from research published in peer-reviewed academic journals.

With each item below, we have also provided some suggestions for you to follow. A more thorough explanation of solutions is provided in a later chapter.

#1: Insensitivity and intolerance of "different"

You might look different from most of your co-workers in physical appearance—tall, short, skinny, overweight, a different sex or gender—and someone gives you a hard time because of it. Or maybe several of your co-workers gang up on you, calling you names, leaving sticky notes with hurtful messages in your work area, or sabotaging your workflow.

Solution: Keep in mind that just because you look different, you don't deserve to be treated differently and should speak up about it. Usually, these "fun" name-calling "games" start with one person. As scary as it might seem, it is important that you walk up to the "funny guy," fake some courage if you have to, and let him know that you do not find that remark funny *or* acceptable. This is your workplace as much as anyone else's and you come here to work, not to get harassed. Ask him to refrain from such remarks in the future.

The new girl

Gabby was a professional through and through. And when she started her new job, she just couldn't believe how loose the rules were. People, including the CEO, came and went as they pleased, there was no corporate policy handbook, and everyone dressed in jeans and t-shirts. To a woman who had been dressing in suits and working a strict eight-hour day her entire life this was very strange.

After awhile, everyone was picking on her and she started to really despise going to work. Out-casted and ignored, she was being bullied (i.e., mobbed) by most of her peers.

In talking with her friends outside of work about her situation, she came to realize the problem: by wearing suits and working a firm eight-hour work day she was going against the grain. The other employees must've been worried that, due to her behavior, the CEO would decide to enforce stringent rules and start requiring business attire and clocking in. She was threatening their way of life.

Gabby had to make a choice. She could relax and try to fit in, or move on to a new company more fitting for her. She decided to loosen up and try to make it work – and it did. As she made an effort to do things the way they'd always been done in this workplace, her peers stopped fearing her, and began to accept her as one of them.

Also consider whether you are dressing differently or appear to stand out with your behavior or communication style, such as being too verbose and humorous in a predominantly quiet and somber environment. Someone who goes against "the way it is around here" can feel threatening to employees who have been there for a while and have become used to life being a certain way.

If you are a new employee, for example, one of the biggest challenges you face as the new person is the challenge of fitting in to "the way it is." Of course, it seems like they should just accept you for who you are—you shouldn't have to try to fit in because you are the most qualified for the position. But, that's not the way new jobs work. Fitting in to the culture is just as important as your performance. Anytime a new person joins the team they threaten the "way it is" and therefore may be under a microscope until everyone feels comfortable.

As much as you want to impress with your performance, be sure that you are focusing on becoming a collaborative team member too.

#2: Someone thinks you make too many mistakes or are an underperformer

You do not have to make a mistake to be the target of the "screw-up police." They are watching like hawks to catch you making the smallest error. When you do make one, they will yell at you as if it were the error of the century. But these people are so committed to their aggressive ways that they'll torment others even when there's no actual mistake. You may find yourself being accused of mistakes you definitely were not responsible for, or being blamed for mistakes that didn't even actually happen.

In addition to mistakes you make here and there at work (and we all make them because we are human), many bullies will accuse you of being an underperformer whether you actually are one or not. Unfortunately, a common misconception among human resource professionals is that targets of bullying are indeed underperformers who can't take the heat when their boss puts pressure on them to perform better. While this might be the case once in awhile, most of the time targets are really excellent performers and bullies are threatened by their ability to excel. But in the eyes of human resources, it couldn't possibly be the manager who is misbehaving.

Research conducted by the Workplace Bullying Institute in 2007 found, for example, that in 44% of cases where bullying was reported the employer did nothing, and in 18% of cases the employer worsened the problem for the target. Furthermore, 24% of respondents claimed they were terminated or driven out and 13% indicated they transferred departments, while only 9% of bullies were punished and 14% of bullies were terminated. These numbers are shocking because they indicate that when the manager is the bully, often it is the target who is held responsible for the bullying.

One favorite bullying tactic is to claim poor performance on an employee evaluation. If you've received several good evaluations, and now, all of a sudden you have a new manager who claims you are a poor performer, certainly you can question the manager, and hopefully the Human Resources Department will be there to back you. But HR could also claim that it is the previous manager who let you get away with underperforming, and that's why you received good reviews in the past. They will tell you this new manager is strictly business, and you will not get away with underperforming any longer.

Most likely the problem is not you or your performance; the problem is the bullying manager. A good manager will tell you immediately when he or she thinks you have done something wrong or are underperforming, and will work with you to come up with a plan to correct the behavior. It is, after all, a manager's job to ensure work is being completed on time and in a quality manner. A bully (or an underperforming manager), on the other hand, will let your seemingly poor performance go until evaluation time. Then the bully will rip you to shreds on the evaluation form and leave you looking bad in the eyes of management. They will also refuse to give you any tools, resources, or information you need to make this alleged and required "performance improvement." In other words, a good manager will help you overcome any areas where you are not performing well; a bully will maliciously use your performance against you.

Solution: Do not allow this behavior to continue any longer. If you're being accused of mistakes all of the time, tell your manager to slow down for a second and listen to you. Let him or her know that this behavior is unacceptable and should stop immediately. If confronting your bully does not get the expected result, or if it makes matters worse, file a report with your superiors. Or... if this is your boss, file a report with the next person up the hierarchy.

If you are being accused of underperformance, gather up all performance evaluations you have received for the last few years. If you do not have them, by most state laws you are entitled to copies of anything in your personnel file, so feel free to ask your human resources department for copies. You do not have to tell them you are building a case against your manager; just let them know you are interested in seeing how you've progressed over the years and would like copies of your performance evaluations.

Send an email to your boss requesting a meeting to discuss your performance and goal-setting for improvement. Be sure you save these emails and the responses you receive, so that you can prove later that you attempted to rectify your own performance by meeting with your manager and attempting to get an understanding of what is expected of you.

If you are successful in securing the meeting, come prepared. Highlight portions of previous reviews that showed your stellar performance, and jot down a list of areas where you feel you are indeed performing well. Remember the goal of the meeting is to find out what goals you need to set for yourself so you can achieve them, not to complain about bullying. This is because goals are tangible, and help you prove you get results.

The goals you set during this meeting should be clear, concise, and include a date of completion. For example, if you were showing up a little late previously, then your goal might be to show up ten minutes early for the next three months, at which time you can checkmark that you achieved that goal, and set a new one for the next three months. If you've been showing up five minutes early, and your boss claimed tardiness was an area in which you needed to improve, then show up fifteen minutes early for the next three months—and even better, why not prove with the punch card or witnesses that you were never late in the first place?! Make sure you keep all documentation related to this meeting, your performance, and your goals—you might need them later.

You might also seek advice from your co-workers, previous bosses, or customers. Ask them if you are a good performer, and ask them to be candid with you about areas you feel you could improve upon. If your manager is saying you are an underperformer, find out what others think and seek to improve in any areas you can.

Finally, just be sure that you continue to perform as a top-rate employee. As frustrated as you might be, don't let the bullying bust your morale and affect your performance. Don't give them something to use against you later. Focus on being a high performer. Shine like the star you know you are.

Katie's story

Katie's boss was full of energy and Katie enjoyed her job—but some co-workers often complained of the boss's bullying ways. Katie didn't feel bullied at all, until one day when she made a mistake on a client's account. The boss sent her a scathing email and copied the entire office so everyone could learn of her horrible mistake.

Katie was annoyed by this behavior and was not about to let her boss bully her. If she let him do it this one time, it would begin the cycle her co-workers complained of. She hit "reply to all" and made no apologies for her mistake. She did, however, offer up five solutions, numbered one by one, and advised her boss that he should tell her which to implement. She also told him that any further discussion about this issue would be behind a closed door.

Immediately after hitting send, her boss came running out of his office and shouted, so that the whole office could hear, "Way to go, Katie! Put the hammer down! I deserved that!"

Katie's approach was successful because she offered solutions. The boss had no choice but to see her as a proactive high producer who'd simply made a mistake. Because of her well thought out solutions, the boss still saw her as an asset, and even appreciated that she'd stood up for herself. She'd nipped the behavior in the bud immediately—something her co-workers had not done effectively.

#3: Someone thinks he or she can get away with being aggressive with you

Bullies behave as badly as they are allowed to behave. Most often, other people you work with are too scared to say anything, or they choose to ignore the behaviors so they can remain productive and out of the bully's way. And, managers and HR don't always see the bullying happening either. If they do, they may choose to ignore it because they don't know how to deal with it, and they probably don't know how damaging it is to you and the organization. So bullies are left to run rampant—but they only run over the people who lie down.

In order to help you determine how assertive you are, we have included an assessment at the end of this chapter.

Solution: It's up to you to stand up for yourself. You must protect yourself and hold the bully accountable for his or her actions. Point out the bully's behavior, and do it in front of other people. During the next staff meeting, try: "Would you please repeat that without yelling? That statement came out pretty sharply, and I'm sure you didn't mean to speak to me like that." Make sure to keep your calm and stand your ground. You can also try a more assertive tactic: "You need to speak to me with more respect—this tone is unacceptable" or, "From now on, when you speak to me, try to be more polite, please." Again, be sure to do this is front of other people—so you have witnesses—and so you have protection. More than likely, the bully will not retort with others in the room. If he does, now you really do have witnesses!

#4: You stand out with superior knowledge or as a top performer

Are you really good at what you do? Are you a top performer? Are you an avid reader? Maybe have a degree or two? Are you a walking lexicon? Fact is, some people just feel threatened by the vast knowledge or top performance of others and want to show superiority by making those people feel miserable. This satisfies their own feelings of inferiority and insecurity. In a study by researcher Maarit Vartia (1996), for example, 68% of targets surveyed reported envy was the reason they were bullied, as well as competition for advancement (38%) and competition for attention from superiors (34%).

Solution: If you are someone who is a top performer because that's who you are – then keep going! Be a star, and don't let the person bullying you get in your way.

#5: You are likeable

If you are a positive, outgoing and well-liked person, it's possible incivility has escalated to bullying over time because you haven't said anything about it. Why would you? You are a nice person who doesn't find pleasure in being rude to others. Furthermore, when you are likeable you are a target for people who are not so likeable, or for people who are jealous of how much others seem to respect you. Unfortunately, your good-nature may have worked against you in this instance because in a fast-paced, highly competitive world nice people may finish last.

As authors Gary and Ruth Namie point out in their book, *The Bully at Work: What You Can Do to Stop the Hurt and Reclaim Your Dignity on the Job*, Americans are very focused on themselves and on winning. Competition is the name of the game—not collaboration. Despite possibly hundreds of surveys supporting the notion that interpersonal skills and a "team-player" attitude is highly prized in employees, the fact is a competitive attitude is what earns promotions, bonuses, and safety from layoffs when things are tight.

Solution: We're not saying you should show up to work tomorrow with your game face on prepared to knock down anyone in your way. (That would make you a bully.) What we are saying is that while being a team player is important, and having a positive attitude is valuable to your ability to work with others, pay close attention to your organization's culture. You may find it is important to step out of your comfort zone sometimes and become competitive, assertive, and ready for action. Stand up for yourself, your work product, and your work ethic when you need to. Don't let anyone take that away from you.

#6: You come across as shy or unassertive

Are you soft-spoken and shy? Is it hard for you to vocalize how you feel about something? When you have a good idea are you able to articulate it to a group of co-workers, or do you worry about whether or not people will make fun of your idea or insult you? Unfortunately, shyness is often mistaken for lacking confidence, and bullies are especially attracted to people who are silent because those people give the bully the feeling that they will just take it. If you don't speak up for yourself then you make it easy for them. Remember that whether you mean to or not, your nonverbal communication sends a message to the person interacting with you. If you seem shy, introverted, or unable to stand up for yourself, people might take that as a sign of weakness even if you are the strongest person around.

Solution: Practice speaking up. Look people in their eyes when you speak to them and when they speak to you. You might feel that this is awkward, but being silent and avoiding eye contact is much more awkward in the other person's perception. Essentially, effective communicators are assertive and articulate, they stand up for themselves, and they do not hesitate to speak up when they have an idea to share or believe they are being stepped on. They speak up with grace, passion, and fervor – and the power they exude becomes a shield against people who may initially attempt to target them with childish behaviors.

Think about the boldness you will project when standing with your arms on your hips or down at your side, rather than folded across your chest (a signal of fear or shyness). During an interaction with an aggressive person, point your toes forward, plant both feet firmly on the ground, chest out, chin up, make constant eye contact, and show with your body language that you are not afraid and you know *exactly* what you are talking about. Even if you're scared

---

Building confidence

On "game days," as she calls them (those days she knows extra bravery is required), Amber pulls her hair straight back, pins back the thick bangs that often cover her eyes, puts on one of her brightly colored shirts, and slides into her favorite pair of power pumps. With nowhere to hide she has no choice but to be confident, bold, and daring all day. This helps her carry her head high and speak her mind when she needs to.

---

to death on the inside...they can't see that if you are purposefully displaying confident communication. These slick moves come with courage (even if you have to fake it), practice, and belief in yourself.

#7: You are perceived as a complainer

Are you a fault-finder? If so, you might attract some negative behaviors from people who have bullying tendencies because they may perceive you as a whiner or a downer. If your co-worker or manager is focused on getting things done, a person who seems to be in the way by finding things wrong may be targeted for bullying behaviors.

Solution: Realize that in life, we see what we focus on. But, as they say, "every coin has two sides," and just because you focus on one side, it does not mean that there isn't another one. Make a conscious effort to notice positive things happening, and point them out before you start in on discussing what's wrong. For example, if a co-worker comes up with an idea and you're not so sure it's a good one, tell her that by saying, "This is a neat idea. I think it could work if we… However, some of the problems I see with the idea are…" If you fail to point out what's right with the idea first, you may come off as a complainer. In other words, when you notice problems voice your observation—but not as criticism, complaints, or whining. Instead, voice it as an objective observation.

#8: You are a whistleblower

Because executives understand the value of receiving information that comes "from the trenches," many organizations have policies in place to protect employees who speak up when they witness something unethical happening, and even provide anonymous hotlines for the employee to call so they feel comfortable making a report. In addition, Congress has provided legal protections for whistleblowers in a variety of areas, including the reporting of sexual harassment or harassment, misuse of property, or manufacturing processes that threaten the safety of consumers, to name just a few. The fact that policies and laws exist to protect whistleblowers indicates that the government and most organizations recognize that whistle-blowing can result in retaliation—often in the form of bullying (yet bullying is not recognized as illegal).

In a survey report released by the Ethics Resource Center (ERC) in 2010, for example, the ERC found that 15% of employees who reported misconduct perceived retaliation as a result of their actions. Six in ten reported a cold shoulder, exclusion from decisions and important work activities, and verbal abuse by someone in management. More than four in ten respondents reported that they almost lost their jobs, were verbally abused by other employees, and were denied promotions or raises. Almost three in ten reported that they were relocated or reassigned to a new position, while two in ten reported that they were demoted.

Solution: You made the decision to exhibit stellar and ethical behavior, and now you are being retaliated against. This is clearly unfair. Unfortunately, your actions have made life hard for the person or people you reported, and while they brought this on themselves by choosing to be unethical in the first place, they of course blame you for bringing it to the attention of management or a government agency. As we know from personal experience, college teachers experience the same retaliation when a student earns an F in their class. Of course, the student sees the F as the teacher's fault, and may even report the teacher to the Dean. In their mind, the teacher is the reason they received an F—it couldn't possibly be their poor study habits or inability to attend class regularly! For them, retaliation against the teacher is the way to take back control. It makes the F easier to swallow when they rationalize that it wasn't their fault, and the same goes for the bullies who are angry that their behavior was reported.

As we have and will continue to say throughout this book, if you are being bullied and not receiving the support you need from management, then consider taking another job elsewhere. This is obviously not fair to you—why should *you* have to leave? You haven't done anything wrong. But you must protect yourself and your health. If the unethical conduct you reported, and the resulting retaliation, is not being addressed, do you really want to work there?

If faced with witnessing unethical conduct in the future, the first thing you should do is assess the situation. One factor to take into consideration when deciding to whom you should report misconduct is your organization's culture. If the importance of ethics and ethical behavior is a strong message coming down from the top, then you can feel safe that making a report will be seen as a valuable contribution. On the other hand, if your organization is allowing bullying to occur, we might be safe assuming that ethics isn't a strong part of your organization's culture. You may also consider the way previous reports were handled. If you are aware of other employees who reported misconduct, consider how the report was handled and investigated, and whether that employee was retaliated against or not.

#9: You are dealing with past experiences or present happenings

Many of the targets of bullying we have talked to have expressed life situations in their past or present that have left them feeling scared, hurt, or depressed. Unfortunately, if these wounds never heal they can turn into a communication style that makes it easy for bullies to target. These personal experiences are private matters, but don't let the bully use them against you.

Some targets of bullying might go through a traumatic personal event that triggers bullying as a result of the loss of focus on work. One individual we spoke to, for example, received news of cancer and after a long battle and time off from work, she returned to work victorious and cancer free. Only three days after returning to work, she learned her husband had a heart condition. A few months later, the heart condition worsened and caused his death. Through all this, her boss remained un-empathetic and told her to "get over it" and accused her of "milking the system." Eventually this individual was bullied right out of her job.

Just as there are laws that prevent retaliation for whistle-blowing, there are also laws that prevent companies from firing employees when they or their family members get sick. In this situation, the time off to deal with her own sickness and the sickness of her husband was allowed—but only at the cost of constant belittling and criticism. This drove the target into further depression and ultimately resulted in her quitting and forfeiting her seniority within a government agency. Sadly, this individual will likely have a hard time trusting managers in the future, and these experiences will probably make her a target of bullying in future positions.

There have also been some connections made between targets of bullying as children and targets of bullying as an adult. Researchers Smith, Singer, Hoel and Cooper found in their 2003 study that children who have a hard time coping with bullying at school might possibly be at risk for future problems in their workplaces. They found that 20% of their respondents who had been a victim in school were more likely to be bullied at work. However, that number also means many (around 80%) targets of bullying in school are not bullied at work.

Solution: Take care of yourself. Do what you need to do to become emotionally healthy again and end any pain you may be feeling from previous experiences. No job is worth the additional pain and trauma being added on every time you deal with a bullying co-worker. If you haven't already, seek counseling from someone who can help you move forward and rebuild your confidence and life.

#10: You have rationalized your co-worker's behavior as acceptable

As trainers and keynote speakers who have spoken all over our nation and in other countries, we have found that some audience members are in shock after the presentation is over. "I think I've been bullied," they say, or "I am pretty sure my last boss was a bully now that you've explained it." These are individuals who were mistreated at work but really had no idea it was going on. They've been telling themselves all this time that adults do not abuse each other at work, and that all adults in the workplace are professional. They accepted that the yelling and name-calling was a normal part of daily business. These individuals had rationalized their abuse at work.

Cognitive dissonance describes the sensation we have when our behaviors and our actions do not match up, or when we have conflicting ideas in our heads. It is a mental reaction to feelings of uneasiness, and according to researchers, we have a motivation to reduce dissonance by changing our attitudes or actions, blaming others for our own action (or inaction), or denying that something happened at all. (Guilt is an example of cognitive dissonance, and we usually relieve this dissonance by taking action and apologizing, or convincing ourselves that what we did wasn't that bad. Whatever path we choose, we are seeking to relieve the disconnect between our actions and our feelings, or guilt, also known as cognitive dissonance.)

Being the target of workplace bullying creates cognitive dissonance for you. On one hand, you are a professional. You work hard and seek to be the best you can be and put in a hard day's work. You believe that work is a place where everyone should be supportive and respectful of each other. You rely on your paycheck to pay your bills, because, after all, you have rent or a mortgage and mouths to feed. On the other hand, you are severely mistreated at work. Each day you are yelled at, abused, manipulated, and made fun of. Despite your hard work, you are mistreated. How can this be? How can it be that someone is simply so awful and uncaring? How can a person treat others with such disdain? Your thoughts about yourself, your workplace, and your actual experiences don't match. You have cognitive dissonance.

Because your situation doesn't make any sense, you have internal conflict. Your mind is motivated to reduce the dissonance by adjusting your thoughts about yourself or your situation. You can't leave your job and the managers don't seem to care, so that leaves you with no other option to reduce dissonance but to rationalize that the bullying is normal or that you did something to deserve it.

Solution: Picking up this book or doing any research at all on your situation is a sign that you no longer believe the bullying behavior is rational. You now understand that what is happening on the job is *not* normal or okay, and you can do something about it. Now you are reducing your dissonance by claiming the bullying behavior is inappropriate and that you should do something about it, and that's the healthy route to take.

#11: You are in a new job

If you were recently transferred to a new department, got promoted, or got a new job you might end up working side by side with someone who is bitter about why you got that job or promotion, or bitter for a number of other reasons unrelated to you. This person might pick on you to unload their frustrations. In addition, because you are in a new place, there's a good chance you are working really, really hard to show your boss that you can do all of the things you said you could during the interview process. This is just one more reason for the person bullying you to single you out—you're simply attempting to be one of the top performers or maybe just trying to blend in. Either way, you are new at this place, and you've done nothing to deserve this treatment.

Solution: If a new coworker or manager raises his or her voice at you or attempts to become aggressive, keep your calm, stand up straight, look 'em straight in the eye, and state that it is not necessary to yell at you. Express that you respond much better to professional communication than to yelling.

§

In conclusion, please note that the reasons you might be a target that we have provided in this chapter are general, and although we have tried to identify as many as possible for you, nothing in human behavior is 100%. The problem is that targets, bullies, and organizations all have certain characteristics that, when stewed up together just right, create an environment where bullying can flourish and thrive.

We all adopt certain behaviors and communication styles because we have found they work for us. Some have found that if they are nice to others and supportive, they feel a sense of peace and fulfillment. These people found that their approach works, and they are able to develop great lasting relationships with those around them. Others have found that if they stick to the bottom line, don't waste too much time on small talk, and put in 100% into accomplishing their tasks, they feel the satisfaction of accomplishments and gain the respect of those around them. Still others may have discovered that abusive behavior gives them what they seek—whether it's perceived respect or that others see them as superior. We can't explain every rhyme or reason that someone would become aggressive or learn to gain pleasure out of hurting others. For those of us who seek to be civil and respectful in all of our interactions, this just doesn't make any sense, nor should we have to live with it.

How assertive are you?

Answer the following questions to determine how assertive you are. The questions are hypothetical, which means the situation posed may not exactly emulate situations you will come across at work. In that case, just answer the question as you think you might if you were actually in the situation.

1. A peer asks you to cover his shift tomorrow night, but you already have plans for dinner with your friends. The dinner is just a get together, there is no special occasion planned. Do you:
    a) Explain that you would be happy to do it another time, but you already have plans.
    b) Agree to do it, but ignore him for the next few weeks to send the message that you were upset about working for him.
    c) Agree to cover his shift because it's easier than saying no.

2. Your aggressive boss asks you to complete a project. The instructions are not very clear, so you're not entirely sure how to complete the project. Do you:
    a) Approach your boss with specific questions in order to gain the clarification you need to do the project right.
    b) Ask a co-worker if they can give you additional information on the project.
    c) Do the project as best you can and hope it is completed in the way your boss wanted.

3. An employee from another department comes into your work area to point out a mistake that someone in your department made. The employee is pretty angry because it's affected a customer account and caused her some extra work. You know

118

it wasn't you who made the mistake. How do you handle the conversation?

a) You attempt to understand how the mistake happened and let her know you will talk to your co-workers so as to avoid the mistake in the future.

b) You tell the employee you know who it was and ask her to come back when that person returns from lunch.

c) You apologize for the mistake and say that it won't happen again.

4. When someone cuts in front of you in line in the workplace cafeteria, you:

a) Explain to him that he cut in front of you and acknowledge it was probably an accident.

b) Say nothing and shoot him glares whenever you think he might notice.

c) Say and do nothing.

5. You shared a great idea with your boss, who in turn asks you to discuss your idea during the company meeting on Friday. There will be 50 people there. What is your response?

a) Agree to make the presentation, prepare your notes in the days before the meeting, and present your idea.

b) Agree to make the presentation, prepare your notes in the days before the meeting, but also lose a lot of sleep in the days before the meeting.

c) Respectfully tell your boss that you'd prefer not to, and ask him to share the idea on your behalf.

6. You generally like your fellow employees, but one of them tends to spend a lot of the workday talking. You and co-

workers all agree is really distracting from your work. Moving forward, you will:

a) Pull the employee into your office and politely tell him that sometimes he gets to talking a little too much, and it can be distracting.

b) Try to look busy when he approaches and hope he gets the hint.

c) Stop what you're doing and listen when he talks because you don't want to be rude.

7. When you attend networking events for your industry, you tend to:

a) Talk to people you have never met easily, and usually make a lot of contacts.

b) Hang out near the people you already know, but if someone you don't know approaches you, you will chat with them.

c) Avoid talking to anyone you don't already know.

8. You are a manager, and one of your employees, who is usually on time, has started to come in late. You:

a) Pull him into your office after the third time to let the employee know you've noticed the tardiness and find out why he is late.

b) Pull him into your office after the seventh or eighth time—after all, he'd never been late before so you thought he'd just go back to being on time on his own.

c) Don't say anything at all. After a full three weeks of being late, you terminate his employment.

9. You already have a lot of work to finish before your day is over, and your aggressive boss has just shown up with another

job for you to complete before you leave. Your boss demands the job be completed, as well as everything else, before you call it a night. You:

a) Describe to your boss that you don't think it can all be done before the day is over. It's already 3:00 pm, and he's just added four more hours to your workload, so you insist that he tell you which of the projects can be completed the following day.

b) You take on the work and ask a co-worker to help you out to be sure it's completed.

c) You take on the work, and work pretty much all night to make sure it's complete before morning.

10. You make a mistake at work, and your boss comes barreling down the hall yelling at you at the top of her lungs and in front of all of your co-workers. You:

a) Stand up out of your chair, tell your boss that you realize you made a mistake, and offer three solutions that you can provide in order to rectify it.

b) Apologize to your boss for the mistake and tell her it will never happen again.

c) Provide your boss with an excuse.

11. During a staff meeting, your manager sparks a discussion about an issue. You speak up with an idea about how to resolve it. Several staff members and the boss respond by dismissing the idea quickly, without letting you explain. You:

a) Say, "Hey wait a minute! Hear me out!" and then go on to provide more details about your idea and why it might work.

b) Laugh at yourself and agree it was a silly idea but you were just trying to think outside of the box.

c) Say nothing and just keep quiet for the rest of the discussion.

12. You have vacation planned for next week, and are looking forward to some well-deserved and greatly needed time off with your family. The company gets a new client so they ask you to push your vacation back by three days in order to get the client account moving before you're gone for a week. You:
   a) Let them know you'll leave clear instructions with your co-workers about how to move forward, and you will be happy to call in on the first couple days so you don't leave them hanging.
   b) Let them know to call you anytime, and then "forget" to answer your phone and "have computer problems" so you can't check your email. When you return, you tell your co-workers you didn't know you'd be so out of range.
   c) Postpone your vacation, as requested.

13. When you are in an argument, you prefer to:
   a) Work through the conflict until it is resolved. By offering up several solutions and ideas for resolution, as well as listening carefully to the other person, you're bound to work through it.
   b) Agree to whatever the other person wants—it's easier and less time consuming.
   c) Avoid the conflict as much as you can; you're sure eventually it will be forgotten.

14. You heard from one co-worker that another co-worker has been telling everyone lies about you. The co-worker has spread rumors that you are going through a divorce and

management thinks it's really affecting your performance so might fire you. This rumor is nowhere near the truth. You:

a) Ask the co-worker to meet with you, at which time you explain that you don't know if it's true or not, but this was the rumor you heard about, and you wanted to talk about it and make sure you set the record straight.

b) Start spreading rumors about the co-worker yourself. Maybe people will stop thinking and talking about your rumor and start thinking and talking about the one you spread.

c) Do nothing—after all, you can't verify the rumor is being spread, and who cares anyway.

15. You are a manager and have set appointments with each of your employees to discuss performance and future goals. One employee shows up 45 minutes late to the meeting without any real explanation. You:

a) Mention to the employee, politely, that this is not a good way to start off a goal-setting meeting with the boss.

b) You don't say anything at the start of the meeting, but during the discussion make an under-the-radar kind of comment about the slip-up.

c) Don't say anything at all—the employee is usually at meetings on-time anyway.

16. Your co-worker pokes fun at you sometimes in front of others, making sarcastic comments and calling you names. It's supposedly all in fun, and it's nothing too derogatory or offensive, but it still bothers you. You:

a) Ask the co-worker politely to stop doing that because it's unprofessional and you find it offensive.

b) Start poking fun back. When he makes a snide comment, you retort with something equally sarcastic.

c) Say nothing. It's not that big of a deal anyway because it's not like sexual harassment or hostility; it's just all in fun.

SCORE: Now tally up how many A's, B's and C's you marked.

A: _____   B: _____   C: _____

If you marked mostly A's:

You are assertive. You're good at speaking up for yourself, and you understand how important it is to do so with professionalism. Assertiveness is a positive communication skill. When you speak up for yourself in a polite and overt way, it results in building self-esteem and maintaining a positive relationship with others.

If you marked mostly B's:

You are passive-aggressive. This means that you choose to stand up for yourself in a manner that is covert, or "under-the-radar." You try to let people know you are bothered by their actions, but you attempt to do so in a way that some might consider sneaky or unprofessional. This is dangerous because people will begin to believe you cannot be trusted. It might be time to reconsider how you go about taking action. It is better to be clear and concise with others by stating what you need, rather than playing tricks or doing things that can be misconstrued. How can your needs be met if you're not being clear about what they are?

If you marked mostly C's:

You are avoidant of standing up for yourself. It's easier for you to just let things go and try to move past them without talking them over. You are being unfair to yourself because you are not getting your needs met, and you are likely seen as someone who allows others to "walk all over them." Eventually, you will begin to become very frustrated with the fact that people take advantage of you, and your self-esteem will be severely affected, if it hasn't been already. Consider using the tips provided in this book to become more assertive. If you are seen as assertive, it becomes more unlikely that you will be bullied.

CHAPTER 5: NOW WHAT?

Twenty-three tools to end bullying

At this point, you have learned myths of workplace bullying, the levels of workplace bullying, why people resort to bullying, and why you might be targeted. So far, we have provided helpful tips and pieces of information that you might need in order to successfully battle the bullying. This chapter, however, is a comprehensive compilation of practical strategies we know you will find useful when dealing with your nemesis.

#1: Acknowledge and name the problem

The very first step in dealing with aggressive and damaging behaviors in the workplace is to acknowledge that there is a problem and give it a name. Once we know that there's something going on, it is important to identify that "something" and name it.

Some people feel that "bullying" is a childish term and are reluctant to use it in describing adult behaviors. The bottom line is, however, that it is important to give the behaviors a name; and since we are dealing with actions that are intended to humiliate, belittle, manipulate, or intimidate others, "bullying" is just the perfect (and widely accepted) term to describe them collectively.

Finding the language to describe your situation is important because language allows you to understand your own reality or what is really going on. Having the right vocabulary to describe and explain what's happening at work during self-talk and when talking to others is an extremely powerful first step in the process of overcoming bullying at work.

#2: Confront the person bullying you

Your chances of success go up if you confront the person as soon as the first or second incident surfaces.

We must caution you that confronting an aggressive person can backfire. If you confront this person, he or she may see it as an attack and increase the abusive behavior. If you confront the person in front of others it may be seen as disrespectful, but if you do it one-on-one you have no witnesses. So confront with caution. Use the assertiveness tips we provide in this book, and avoid blaming or finger-pointing. Just respectfully point out that the behavior is inappropriate and hurting your ability to be effective.

Stay calm; be professional. If the other person responds with aggression, say, "Jim, I'm not here to argue. I just simply want you to stop _____ (insert the unwanted behavior here), Jim. I treat you with respect, and I expect the same from you. Jim, starting today, please refrain from _____."

Notice a few things about these statements. We've used the individual's name, Jim, several times. Using a person's first name like this is a form of assertiveness. It puts a person on the spot and usually gets a person to take notice and actually listen. (Think about the old trick parents use when they catch their children doing something wrong: They call them by their first, middle, and last name because it gets attention and implies dominance. The same applies here.)

Also notice that we purposefully avoided labeling Jim as a "bully" in the example. Since your goal is to stop the behavior, do not antagonize the person who is bullying you by sinking to their level and calling them names. Calling anyone names is called *evaluative language,* and you want to use *descriptive language*. Descriptive language means that you describe the behavior that is bothering you in detail, as we did above in our example. It's just a simple twist in word choice, but it's a powerful one during conversations with someone who is bullying you.

#3: Avoid name-calling

Even though it is important to recognize what's going on—you are being bullied at work—it is also important to understand that you are facing a human being who is not a bully but rather a person adopting bullying behaviors. Saying, "he is a bully" gives the individual more power over you because in your mind you accept that you are facing a person whose every interaction with you will be negative. If he is a bully, you cannot do anything about it. "He is bullying me" is a subtle but powerful shift in your situation. Now you have made the claim that this individual is exhibiting an undesired behavior, and you can perhaps change it.

Language allows you to control your reality. The language you choose to describe an event, situation, or person is important. Your language choice determines your perception of your situation and your perception of whether or not it's changeable. What we are talking about here is empowering language. *Empowering language* gives you control and options. *Disempowering language*, on the other hand, leaves you feeling like a victim.

We know at first read this idea might seem silly. You might be thinking, "Who cares how I say it! He makes me feel bad, I'm

> **Empowering vs. disempowering language**
>
> Example of Empowering Language: *"My coworker displays some bullying behaviors—I am going to tell her to stop it."*
>
> Example of Disempowering Language: *"She is bullying me. I feel like there's nothing I can do."*

129

stressed, and I'm scared to death at work every day—and that's what I care about!" But trust us, these language nuances are part of the first important steps in taking control of how you are treated at work.

#4: Focus on yourself and your actions, not on the bullying

We tend to focus a lot on bullies when we are being harassed by them, almost obsessively in many cases. This is allowing the bully to win because instead of focusing on how to overcome bullying, you are focusing on how bad the individual makes you feel. Try to focus on yourself, your work, your own behavior, and how well you're doing. Make a conscious choice to push the bullying out of your mind.

It's easy to say that our thoughts and emotions are not a choice, but that simply isn't true. *You have control over what you think about; what you think about does not have control over you.* You have control over your thoughts. Understanding that will help you take control of how you feel, and you'll be able to face your bullying coworker.

At the end of the work day, for example, you might drive home thinking about how horrible you were treated that day and how unhappy you are at work. You might go over in your head the fact that the individual bullying you had even more wrath than yesterday. What you want to try to think about instead is your own behavior. What could you have done differently? What will you do differently tomorrow? What was your body language like during your interaction with the bully? How will you address the bullying tomorrow? What will you do to make yourself happy and healthy?

It takes a little practice, but taking control of your thoughts is not as hard as it seems.

#5: Take control of your response to the bullying behavior

Believe that you are in power and have control of the situation. As Eleanor Roosevelt once said, "No one can make you feel inferior without your consent."

Remain professional, do a great job all of the time, and disregard attempts to bring you down. You deserve respect in your workplace, but you are responsible for garnering that respect and for projecting a confident and "don't screw with me" image to everyone around you. That means you should command respect for your work and professionalism while at the same time treating everyone the same way, including the person bullying you. Do not allow yourself to be dragged down to the level of an abusive co-worker. Lead by example and remain confident and professional.

Remember, you do have control over your thoughts. You do have control over your own choices. Consider the story of a man whose airplane was shot down over the ocean during his deployment. For three days he floated in the ocean, and in terms of what to think about, he had two options: succumb to his circumstances and start thinking about dying, or focus his thoughts on survival. He chose to think about living. He did live, and was eventually rescued. He also claims that he is a much better person as a result of this experience. He is more positive, a better leader, and more appreciative of his life. Researchers in the field of positive psychology call this Post-Traumatic Growth (PTG), which refers to the fact that after a traumatic experience this individual felt as though he'd grown as a person, and was even glad the universe had given him the chance to do so.

Had he thought about dying, the outcome for him would've have been much different. He very likely could have talked himself into giving up and may have died before he was rescued. If rescued, who he became as a result of that experience would have been much different. Rather than being more positive, he would've been negative and unhappy, blamed others for his problems, and maybe even suffered from Post-Traumatic Stress Disorder (PTSD).

Remember, you can't always control other people or the situation you're in, but you do have control over what's happening in your mind.

#6: Reframe the situation

Reframing is a powerful tool anyone can use in a sticky situation—whether dealing with a nasty co-worker, feeling sad about a child going off to college, or being upset after a breakup.

Reframing is a powerful self-talk communication tool used to change the way you look at a situation or context; because the way you frame a situation or context will have much to do with its outcome. Your perception of the world, frame of reference, or paradigm limits your view of the world because it defines what you see. When you take time to question your initial perception, or take time to analyze and question your beliefs, you will open yourself up to see the world differently—you will see possibilities for change and growth that you might not have noticed before.

When you look out of the window frame on the right side of your office, for example, you might see the alleyway with garbage scattered throughout the dim and dirty strip, some rats running through, and maybe even a homeless person riffling through the garbage seeking food. How depressing. When you look out of the window frame on the left side, you might see trees, the neighborhood park, a pond with ducks, and a family picnicking in the grass enjoying the sunshine. Which window frame do you prefer to look through?

You can go to work every day looking out of the "victim window" and having as your frame of reference a situation where you have no control. Or, you can go to work each day looking through the "active, confident, and strong-willed window" where you're in control. Now you are someone who sees the bullying as a challenge, a character builder, and a situation that once overcome will make you a better and stronger person. Once you start reframing negative situations around you, the possibilities for change start to shine through, like sunshine rays penetrating your window on a beautiful, sunny day.

So how does changing your perception of a situation make a real difference? It certainly doesn't change the fact that you are stuck with a coworker who is a real jerk. Think about the story of Victor Frankl, a neurologist and psychiatrist, who ended up in concentration camps during World War II. Through his educated eyes, he watched as people in the camps died all around him while others lived, although they looked as though they shouldn't have made it. What he realized through his interactions with these people was that the difference between those who died of starvation and those who did not had nothing to do with their health or body strength; it had everything to do with their attitude—the way they *chose* to look at their situation. Most of the people who believed they would make it through their hunger and starvation did indeed. Of the people who believed they were going to die of hunger and starvation, most did.

Now we ask you—if those people, living in as close to hell as one can possibly be, were able to reframe their situations into one that made them stronger and allowed them to survive, can't you? According to Frankl, " . . . the last of human freedoms is to choose one's attitude in any given set of circumstances, to choose one's own way."

#7: Build up your confidence

Steven R. Covey, author of *7 Habits of Highly Effective People*, says we should, "Begin with the end in mind." That means when you go to work, you should visualize how you'll interact with your bullying co-worker and what the end result of the conversation will be. Visualize yourself standing up to him or her. In addition, use affirmations to build up your confidence. Affirmations have proven to be very effective at transforming our feelings and actions.

Start your days off in the mirror with the affirmations, "I am awesome, I am terrific!" Heck, even while you're at work, close your office door or step outside a few times and say your affirmations. Yours might be: "I'm brave, I'm in control, I deserve respect!" With a little faith, those words can turn your workplace ordeal and whole life around.

Faith develops and increases through repetitive affirmation. If you attend church, for example, there's a good chance your faith is nurtured each time you go. The more information you receive, the more your certainty about your faith is confirmed. If you stop going to church, loss in faith may result. The same happens when we stop believing in ourselves.

So head to the *Church of You* each morning and stand in front of the mirror to shout your personal affirmations ("I am terrific! I am great at my job! I will overcome the bully! I am not a helpless victim!"). The more you say it, the more you feel it; the more you feel it, the more you believe it; the more you believe it, the greater your courage becomes; the greater your courage becomes, the closer you are to reaching your goal of overcoming bullying.

Facing challenges takes courage; you find that courage through persistence in your positive thinking and attitude. You have the determination and doggedness to fight; and you find it within yourself by consistently reaffirming it.

Here are some examples of positive affirmations:

- I am awesome at the work I do!
- I am confident!
- I can stand up to anyone who tries to disrespect me!
- I feel great!
- I am happy, intelligent, and courageous!
- I am worth my weight in gold!
- I am stronger and stronger every day!

Write out positive affirmations

Consider some positive affirmations you could use in the morning to get your confidence-booster going:

_____

_____

_____

_____

_____

_____

_____

_____

#8: Focus on building up your self-esteem

As you already know, your self-esteem is at risk when in a bullying situation. That means it is extremely important that you focus on keeping it intact. Doing this is no easy feat, but here are some simple things you can do to get started:

- Jot down all of the things you have achieved and are proud of. Celebrate your successes.
- Set some small goal for yourself and achieve it. Then set another one, and achieve it. Repeat.
- Exercise. It can help you burn off some of that energy or anxiety you're feeling—and of course it's good for you in lots of other ways too.
- Teach yourself a new skill, or join a class in order to learn something new. Join a martial arts club, ballroom dancing, or a yoga class; join an indoor rock-climbing group, or learn to play an instrument—engage in something that provides you with satisfaction and a sense of accomplishment.
- Join a crowd of people doing some good—become an active member of a volunteer organization, church, or professional association, for example.

#9: Maintain conscious awareness of your body language at all times

When our self esteem is in the dumps, we are feeling beat up, or are unhappy, it shows in our body language. Equally, when we feel great, confident, and happy, our body language says it all.

Next time you have an argument with your children (or you see someone arguing with their children), for example, watch how their body language changes as they start to realize they have lost the argument and will be grounded for the weekend. Your child will likely go from puffed up in the chest and chin up, to arms folded and shoulders hunched over.

The same happens to you, too, during conversations with others. How you feel every day at work is communicated through your body language whether you like it or not, and even if you don't speak a word to anyone. The trick, then, is to be aware of your body language so that you can change it accordingly. No matter how you feel, if you use assertive body language it will show others you are confident—and you'll notice that with the assertive body posture, you actually feel assertive.

Think about how you sit the next time you are talking to a person who makes you uncomfortable. Are your arms and legs crossed? Do you look away or down? Is your chin down and are your shoulders hunched over? If you answered yes to these questions, then you are undoubtedly communicating to others that you are feeling closed off, nervous, shy, and not willing to stand up for yourself—even if you don't mean to. All of these nonverbal communication codes show your co-workers, including the bullying ones, that they can trample all over you—that you are not prepared to stand up for yourself or your beliefs.

> ### Assertive body language
>
> - Sit or stand up straight and lean forward slightly
> - Keep feet planted firmly on the ground
> - Keep toes pointed forward at all times
> - Put your hands on your hips or down to the side instead of folded across your chest
> - Keep firm eye contact as you speak, and as the other person replies
>
> Also be sure to:
> - Use an assertive tone of voice—make sure you don't whisper or come across as complaining
> - Be factual and to the point
> - Use the bully's first name a lot

Next time someone bullies you, focus on your "battle stance." Hold your chin up, lean forward slightly, toes pointed forward, hands on hips or at your side, and deliver firm extended eye contact. If the verbal torrent goes on, tilt your head slightly, almost like saying, "I can't believe you have the audacity to speak to me like this." This body language shows others that you are confident and ready to stand up for yourself. This is a way to subtly confront aggressive people at work by showing that you are not someone to mess with—without saying a single word. It shows the other person you are ready to stand up for yourself, but it also helps you develop the courage to actually do so. You are what your body language says you are.

#10: Be aware of your conflict management style

Before we start in on conflict management, it is important to note that bullying is not conflict. Conflict happens when two people disagree on an issue, and when each party perceives that the other party is standing in the way of their needs. Bullying, on the other hand, is psychological abuse. Bullying occurs when one party has overpowered the other. But we bring up conflict management style because, although bullying is not conflict, your conflict management style and that of the bully's play a factor in how a bullying scenario plays out.

Since the 1970s, the Thomas-Kilmann Conflict Mode Instrument, also known as the TKI, has been a widely accepted model for describing conflict management styles. Created by Kenneth Thomas and Ralph Kilmann, the model asserts that we exhibit one of five conflict management styles as a result of two possible focuses during conflict: our own needs, or the other person's needs. People who focus strictly on their own needs during conflict are likely very aggressive, and people who focus only on the other person's needs are likely avoiding conflict or prefer to accommodate that other person. According to the model, in order for everyone to resolve the conflict with a win-win outcome, both parties should focus on collaborating or compromising through appropriate levels of assertiveness.

> ## The five conflict management styles
>
> *Competing:* Aggressive and focused on own needs, and on winning.
>
> *Avoiding:* Avoids conflict whenever possible. Usually not willing to discuss resolutions, and prefers just to try to "let it go."
>
> *Accommodating:* Agree with the other person just to keep the peace, or because they fear having a disagreement.
>
> *Compromising:* Seeks solutions to the problem that involve some kind of middle ground. Both parties may need to give something up in order to get something amicable in return.
>
> *Collaborating:* Focused on meeting everyone's needs, reaching a consensus, and finding a solution with which all parties involved are happy.

The first type of conflict style, *competing*, is what workplace bullies exhibit. This means that they are aggressive, uncooperative, focused on their own needs, want to win or get their way all of the time, and don't take interest in the people with whom they are in conflict. They are people who completely lack empathy or concern for other people's feelings. This is clearly a win-lose situation—the bully wins, you lose.

The second conflict management style, *avoiding*, means exactly that. An individual who demonstrates a conflict avoidant style is quick to avoid engaging in conflict altogether. This might be the conflict style you, as the target, subscribe to. The avoiding conflict management style is generally considered lose-lose. When one party avoids conflict, both parties lose out on the opportunity to resolve it.

When things get too tense in a bullying situation, avoiders often show inward body language, with arms folded, head down, and lack of eye contact. When a person yells, avoiders choose to just "take it" rather than stand up for themselves or speak their mind. Most people who are conflict avoiders do so because they fear conflict in some way. In a romantic relationship, this type of conflict management style can be seen as simply not caring about the other person or the outcome of the issue. In workplace bullying, this type of conflict management style is seen by the bullying coworker as a green light to keep up the abuse.

Accommodating, the third type of style, is the opposite of competing. Accommodators most often agree with the other party just to keep the peace. Much like *avoiding*, an accommodating conflict management style gives abusive co-workers or managers the go ahead to keep backing people into a corner. While avoiders will simply walk away and avoid conflict altogether, the accommodator will put up a bit of a fight but eventually give in. Just like the competing conflict management style, accommodating is also considered win-lose. Again, the bully wins, and the accommodator loses because the accommodator is willing to go along with what the bully wants.

Compromising, the fourth kind of conflict style, involves a moderate level of concern for one's own needs and the needs of the other. Compromising can be a very healthy way to deal with conflict because all parties get some of their needs met, but often at the expense of letting other, hopefully less important, needs go. Usually bullying situations do not involve compromising. Bullies are generally not willing to compromise, and if you've offered up solutions that may result in compromise, chances are the bully wasn't willing to accept the suggestions.

Stop avoiding and accommodating

Use this space to think about your last conversation with a person exhibiting workplace bullying behaviors. Jot down your answers to the following questions:

What was the conversation about?

_____

_____

What was I doing that indicated to the other person that I was being avoidant or accommodating?

_____

_____

What could I have done differently to ensure that the other person didn't see me as a conflict avoider or accommodator?

_____

_____

The fifth and most healthy type of conflict management is *collaboration*. Collaborators focus on reaching a consensus or solution everyone can be happy with.

Now, we understand that compromising or collaborating with bullies may be difficult if they are unwilling to change their own conflict management style. Nevertheless, start focusing on being more assertive and adopt a collaborative conflict management style with everyone around you. While this might not eliminate the bullying altogether, it is a great first step towards showing your bullying coworker that he or she can't just run over you (versus if you adopted the avoidant or accommodating conflict management styles, which will always result in a win-lose outcome for you). At the very least, we suggest that you focus on *not* falling into a pattern of avoiding or accommodating no matter what—and being assertive is the key to doing that.

#11: Avoid passive language

There are three types of language: aggressive, assertive, and passive.

Aggressive language, or the language used by bullies, is characterized as judgmental or threatening, or even as violating another person's personal or physical boundaries. Aggressive communication can also be manipulative, because the person using aggressive communication knows that he can get his way by "walking over" others. Bullies can also be passive-aggressive, which means attempting to avoid confrontation by being passive but getting what they want by being aggressive. It's underhanded aggressiveness and easy to deny. We've all used this style of communication at one time or another, but bullies may use this behavior all of the time.

Assertive language is the ability to express your opinions and feelings openly and without stepping on other people's toes. Assertive people can state their needs and wants in a way that is persuasive, and allows all parties involved in the interaction to maintain their own self-respect. Assertiveness is dependent upon being in control and having a sense of certainty that your behavior will produce the results you are seeking. Assertive communication is the most healthy for you and your personal and professional relationships.

Passive language, also called deferential language, is based on the hopes of avoiding confrontation. This type of communication appears safe to the user. In reality, passive communicators often suffer from feeling abused and taken advantage of. They never share their feelings or make their personal needs known, and can become frustrated in relationships with others because of this.

Table 5.1, below, provides a comparison of the three types of language:

Aggressive	Assertive	Passive
Do this report right now.	It's important to do this report now because the client needs it before the end of the workday.	It would be nice if you would do the report.
Tell me right now why you're always late.	Let's talk about why you've been coming in late so we can work together to address it.	If we could talk about why you're late, I'd appreciate it.
I don't care what you want; this is how you will do it.	I'd really prefer it if you do it this way because...	I don't care how you do it.
You have to work overtime tonight because I said so.	I'd like you to work overtime tonight. It would really help the team out.	I'm hoping you'll work overtime tonight. Can you?

Table 5.1. The three types of language

As you review this table, note the differences in the use of words. While aggressive language assumes superiority and is full of outright demands, passive language sends the message that you are unsure of yourself and your message. Saying things like, "I would appreciate it if..." and "I'm hoping that..." gives others the opportunity to say to themselves, "It's nice you feel that way, but it's not gonna happen." Assertive language gives the message that you are sure of yourself and your message, but that you are empathetic to others' feelings and points of view.

#12: Use the three steps of assertiveness

Assertiveness is the ability to express your opinions and feelings openly and without stepping on other people's toes. It's not aggressive, and it's not passive. As we mentioned above, it's right in the middle, and a very valuable tool.

Assertiveness is dependent upon being in control, confident, feeling good about yourself, and a sense of certainty that your behavior will produce the results you are seeking. Assertiveness follows three steps:

- validation
- statement of problem
- statement of solution

Validation shows you understand the other person. It doesn't mean you agree with them, just that you are attempting to recognize their side.

For example, saying something like, *"I understand you believe my performance is below par"* will acknowledge the bully's point of view, even if you disagree with it. Rather than dismissing their opinion, you're letting them know you heard them. This does not mean you agree with what was said, it's only a conversation starter that shows that you "heard" what the bully said and you are ready to talk about it.

Statement of problem describes your dissatisfaction, and explains why something needs to change.

For example, *"When you write these negative things on my performance review without giving me information that I can use to increase my performance, it hurts our working relationship and my ability to continue to produce satisfactory work for you. I want to be a good performer, but I need to understand what I am doing wrong in specific terms."*

Statement of solution provides a specific request for a specific change in the other person's behavior.

For example, *"I have received over twenty years of raving reviews through six managers, so clearly there is a disconnect in our relationship because all of a sudden the reviews I receive from you are negative. From now on, I expect that we will work together on any of the areas you think I need to improve in. When are you free to meet with me to discuss this in greater detail and determine tangible goals for me to reach?"*

Here's another example:

Validation: *"John, I know you have worked here for much longer than I have."*

State the problem: *"But this morning in the staff meeting I noticed several times that you were rolling your eyes at other staff members when I was speaking. In fact, at one point when I was talking about a customer you looked right at Mary and mouthed, 'How stupid.' This behavior is unprofessional, and it really undermines my credibility with the rest of the team."*

State the solution: *"If you think that the things I am saying are stupid, please verbalize what the issue is to me right now, or even in front of the group at the next staff meeting so I have a chance to defend myself. But please stop disrespecting me in staff meetings."*

Notice a few things about these statements:
- At no time did we call John a bully or any other name; we left name-calling out.
- At no time did we get emotional or mention anything about feelings. The information provided is all based on

fact. John did roll his eyes, and it does indeed undermine credibility.

- The information provided was specific. The more specific and descriptive you are, the harder it is for the bully to deny it. We also focused on one specific behavior, rather than making a sweeping generalization such as, "You always pick on me in staff meetings."
- At no time did we say, "I think" or "I wish" or "I hope." These phrases are wishy-washy and passive, not assertive. Being assertive means being very clear and concise.
- We finished with the final action item. We made it clear what the result of the conversation should be.

It is very possible in this scenario that John would say, "I didn't roll my eyes or say that to Mary. Calm down and stop making things up. You're being silly and overly sensitive."

Your response, again, needs to be assertive, but not argumentative. Keep the emotions out, and stick to the facts. Your response should be, "John, I know what I saw. I'm not making it up, I'm not being sensitive, and I'm telling you that it needs to stop." Then just walk away. Don't give him a chance to keep arguing with you. If you're feeling especially brave, during the next staff meeting when John rolls his eyes say something in front of the whole group. Or, if you have a friend to turn to among your co-workers, ask him or her to say something in front of the group too. There's power in numbers.

#13: Use "You" language

In the book *Tongue Fu! How to Deflect, Disarm, and Defuse Any Verbal Conflict* by Sam Horn, Horn points out that assertiveness experts often emphasize the importance of using "I" when expressing feelings. It is important to take ownership of your own emotions. You're supposed to say things like, "I don't like it when you take that tone of voice with me." In most situations, it is very important that you express your feelings using "I" so that you don't come across as blaming the other person. Blame causes defensiveness.

The three steps of assertiveness

Think about the last time you were feeling bullied. Use this tool to write out how you could have used the three steps:

Validation: Show you are attempting to understand

_____

_____

_____

Statement of Problem: Describe your dissatisfaction

_____

_____

_____

Statement of Solution: Provide a specific request for change

_____

_____

_____

But that doesn't work with bullies, according to Horn. Their attitude is," I don't care if you don't like my tone!" Or they'll launch a more aggressive attack to get you to back off with something like, "Stop being so dramatic!" So instead of, "I don't like the way you treat me" as you might normally say, try, "You need to work on treating others more professionally." This makes them accountable for their own actions. One word of warning: avoid passing judgment. Saying something like, "You are crazy" does not hold a bully accountable; it only fuels their fire.

This tool, like many of the others presented in this chapter, gives you the opportunity to stand up for yourself without being overtly blatant about it. You aren't attacking the bully; you are simply giving a bit of pushback to let the bully know you will not allow yourself to be targeted.

#14: Deflect criticism

Criticism can really hurt. And while we don't have control over the person criticizing us, we do have control over how we react. The fact is we can learn how to avoid taking it in or allowing it to become a part of our self-concept. In order to do so, it is important to put things in perspective. You can do this by asking questions and using a tool we call "fogging." Both of these tools do require a bit of courage, but will get easier the more you use them. You could even try using them at the grocery store or with other people outside of work to get a little practice.

Anyone who is overly critical has become that way because most people have allowed them to be. When the person has gone on a criticizing rampage, everyone else has more than likely just stood there and taken it. You, on the other hand, can break the cycle by asking questions. Specifically, ask questions that seek more information about the issue and that force the criticizer to come up with a goal for the conversation. For example, your conversation might look like this:

Criticizer: *"You keep doing that report wrong! Just over and over again, always wrong. It's so pitiful. How is it that you keep passing the employee evaluations year after year?! Someone else around here has to see how dumb you are. I can't be the only one who thinks you're an idiot."*

You: *"What is the goal of this conversation? I can only assume the goal here is to have the report done right. Calling me names will not achieve that goal; telling me what is wrong with the report will. So, can you tell me exactly what I am doing wrong? Let's go through this mistake by mistake right now, once and for all, and that way future reports will be to your standards."*

Criticizer: *"I don't have time to train idiots. You should already know how to do your job. Don't expect me to do it for you."*

You: *"Again, what is the goal of this conversation? I'm not asking you to do my job but it is clear that you have certain expectations about the report. So I ask again, what exactly would you like me to do differently?"*

In this example, you're not arguing with the bully, you're not being unprofessional, you are simply asking for clarification. You are putting the burden on the bully to tell you exactly what the problem is and to clarify what the real issue is. You've asked for more negatives so that you can constructively solve the problem and move on. You also haven't left the bully any choice but to answer your questions or walk away out of annoyance that you won't just sit back and be criticized.

In some instances, using a tool called "fogging" might also be useful to deflect criticism. Fogging means that you deflect criticism by agreeing with it. This is a useful tool, when appropriate, because it will catch the criticizer off guard.

Here are some examples:

Criticizer: *"Your tie is so ugly today."*
You: *"Yep, it sure is."*

Criticizer: *"Some of the ideas you had in our meeting this morning were so stupid!"*

You: *"You're right! Think about how stupid Benjamin Franklin looked when he tied a key to a kite string and was running around in the rain. Great things only come from wacky ideas."*

Criticizer: *"Man, you're so lazy!"*

You: *"Us hard workers do get a little lazy sometimes. It happens to the best of us."*

Criticizer: *"When are you getting a new job and leaving this place. Everyone hates working with you."*

You: *"Really? That must be a record! To have every single person who works here hate me. That's pretty cool."*

Note that fogging should only be used when agreeing with the criticism doesn't matter. In the example above about the reports, you wouldn't want to respond to, "You did this report wrong" with, "Yep, I sure did." Now you're admitting that you did do your work incorrectly, and you're showing you don't care. That won't fly when you get into the manager's office and report your grievance. But if someone criticizes your tie or your ability to stand up and share ideas with the team, it doesn't matter if you agree with them. It doesn't hurt your credibility at work, but it does throw off the criticizer.

#15: Use the tools of DISC

Earlier in the book, we provided some basic information about the four personality styles known as the DISC Model. Again, we want to reiterate as we did in that chapter that none of the styles are bad or good—they are just different. When two opposite personalities work together the chance for clamor arises simply because the two have vast differences in personality and communication styles.

Understanding how each style likes to be treated and how they prefer to be communicated with is the key to peaceful communication on the job.

In the following pages, we will provide more information about the four styles and some tips in effectively communicating with them. In Figure 5.1, we have provided a quick summary.

Dominance Style – Fast Paced & Task Oriented

Dominance style people are naturally driven and high energy people who, due to their drive and bulldog-like determination to accomplish their goals, can come across as pushy, blunt, and insensitive. Because they are so focused on achieving goals, they usually dislike chit-chat, listening to personal stories, or long-winded conversations. They like their conversations to be clear, concise, and to the point.

For these reasons, the D-style is perhaps the style that can come across as a bully most often. If things don't go their way, these individuals can easily lose their temper and unload their frustrations on whoever is closest to them.

Of course, most D-style individuals are simply more interested in results than in worrying about the feelings of others. However, if you work for a D-style boss, or you have a D-style coworker or subordinate, there are a few things you can do in order to avoid their outbursts or blunt comments:

1. Don't waste their time with chit-chat, stories, or humor.
2. Stick to job-related conversations.
3. Communicate in short, bottom-line sentences.
4. Try to match their faster pace, at least when you are around them, both in communication and in your actions. (D-style individuals can get frustrated when working with slower-paced co-workers or subordinates.)

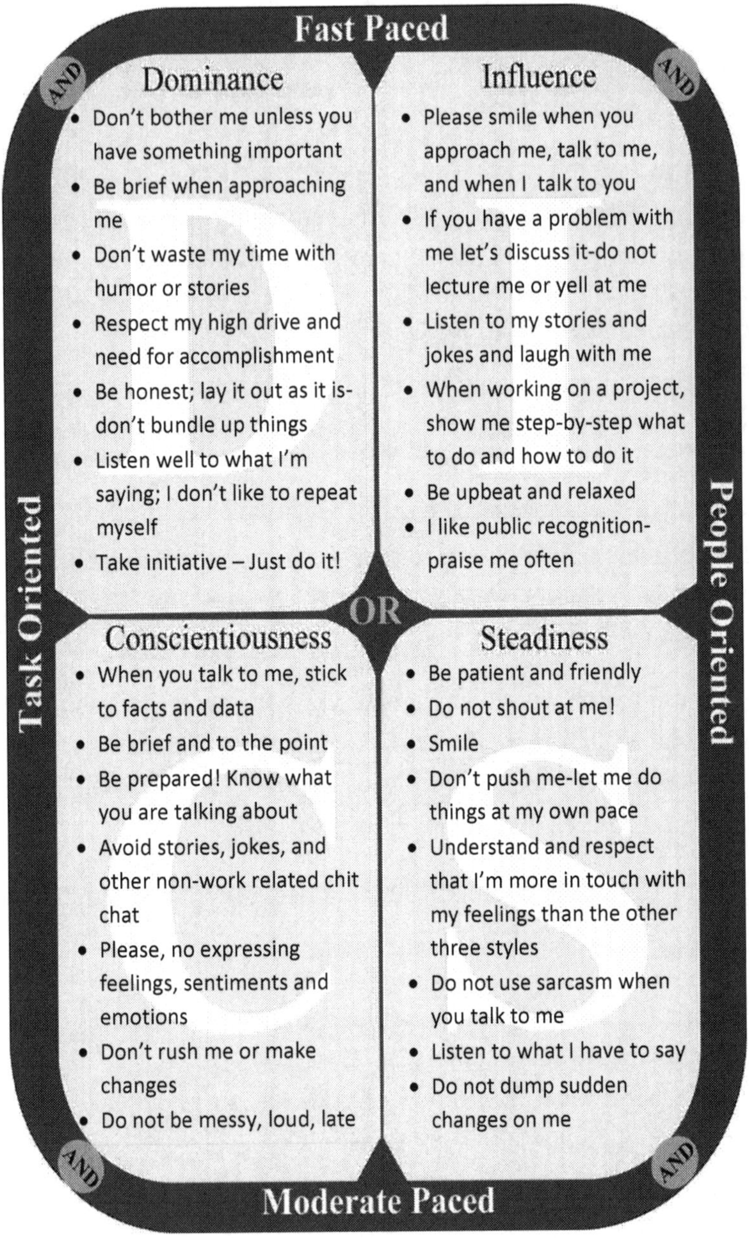

Fast Paced

Dominance
- Don't bother me unless you have something important
- Be brief when approaching me
- Don't waste my time with humor or stories
- Respect my high drive and need for accomplishment
- Be honest; lay it out as it is- don't bundle up things
- Listen well to what I'm saying; I don't like to repeat myself
- Take initiative – Just do it!

Influence
- Please smile when you approach me, talk to me, and when I talk to you
- If you have a problem with me let's discuss it-do not lecture me or yell at me
- Listen to my stories and jokes and laugh with me
- When working on a project, show me step-by-step what to do and how to do it
- Be upbeat and relaxed
- I like public recognition- praise me often

Task Oriented

OR

People Oriented

Conscientiousness
- When you talk to me, stick to facts and data
- Be brief and to the point
- Be prepared! Know what you are talking about
- Avoid stories, jokes, and other non-work related chit chat
- Please, no expressing feelings, sentiments and emotions
- Don't rush me or make changes
- Do not be messy, loud, late

Steadiness
- Be patient and friendly
- Do not shout at me!
- Smile
- Don't push me-let me do things at my own pace
- Understand and respect that I'm more in touch with my feelings than the other three styles
- Do not use sarcasm when you talk to me
- Listen to what I have to say
- Do not dump sudden changes on me

Moderate Paced

Figure 5.1. What the Four Styles Expect of You
(Excerpt from Communication Skills Magic—reprinted with the permission of the author)

5. If you manage a D-style individual, make sure to provide clear rules, goals, and expectations, or else they'll take charge and trample all over your authority.

Most D-style individuals are hard working people who contribute to a team's success; however, when stressed or working with individuals who do not match their pace they can get frustrated and they do not mind bluntly sharing their frustrations.

Influence Style – Fast Paced & People Oriented

Influence style individuals love to influence others with their often great verbal skills. They are fast-paced individuals who love the social aspect of their jobs. I-style individuals will usually do anything in their powers to avoid conflict; however, if they feel disrespected, they can use their verbal skills to punish the "perpetrator."

I-style individuals are usually perceived as friendly, but if for some reason you upset them they can become sarcastic and lash out at you with some degrading and crude humor.

If you work with an I-style coworker, boss, or subordinate, and you feel pushed around or bullied, try the following tips to make the negative behaviors stop:

1. Try to put on a friendly smile when communicating with them. Influence style individuals can often feel stressed when working around people who constantly look too serious.
2. Show (or fake) interest when they tell you stories or jokes; it's the surest shortcut to creating great relationships with an I-style individual (they value highly the social aspect of their workplace).

3. Praise them openly whenever they accomplish something. They love to bask in attention and love recognition for their accomplishments (this is another shortcut to getting on this style's good side).

4. If you have to share technical details, instead of dumping all the data on them, try to share only as much as necessary. If possible, show them what you are talking about as well; this style learns best through hands-on discovery and training. Of the four styles, this style has the shortest attention span and can get frustrated when too many technical details are dumped on them.

5. If your subordinate is an I-style individual, whenever possible provide written instructions of what you expect from them. This style is eager to say, "Yes, I'll do it!" but often will remember only half of what you tell them. Also, they tend to procrastinate, so make sure to follow up regularly on their progress.

I-style individuals are "people" people—they love to have a good time and be on good terms with everyone. However, if they feel disrespected, or if they feel you are not pulling your share of the workload, they'll turn on you and unleash their mighty verbal skills to make you feel their discontent with you or your work.

Steadiness Style – Moderate Paced & People Oriented

Steadiness style individuals love a steady workplace and steady environments in general. They love to know exactly what their job duties are and passionately dislike sudden changes in their work environments or in their work routine. As long as they can work in their routine, they are generally content and productive.

S-style individuals can be the easiest people to get along with. They care very much about the feelings of their co-workers and will do everything possible to avoid conflict and develop great relationships with their co-workers. They'll remain peaceful and smiling even if they have to silently tolerate the insults (perceived or real) of others. However, if their routines are disrupted, and they feel disrespected and unappreciated, they can sabotage workflow by not completing certain tasks (claiming, "it's not in my job description"), work slower than usual, call in sick, or find other ways to hinder productivity and take revenge on whoever ticked them off.

To avoid getting on the rebellious side of the S-style:

1. Smile when you talk to them. Just like the I-style, S-style individuals get stressed when communicating with painfully serious looking individuals.

2. Show patience and don't rush them. S-style individuals are naturally slower paced (and as a result they'll usually provide higher quality outcomes than the Dominance and Influence style co-workers, who value speed over quality).

3. Slow down and listen—that is, really listen. Ask open-ended questions, then smile (or at least do your best not to frown)... and wait for the answer. And don't jump in with follow-up questions; instead, "sit back" and listen.

4. Show your appreciation for their work. Because of their more moderate pace, they are able to pay more attention to details.

5. If your subordinate is a S-style individual, provide clear and detailed description of job related duties. If changes are coming up, make sure to provide detailed reasons why those changes are necessary and HOW those changes will benefit everyone in the organization.

S-style individuals can be the sweetest and most peaceful people on the planet. They love to help others and genuinely care about the feelings and well being of others. However, even this peaceful style can turn on you if they perceive you have stepped on their toes.

Conscientiousness Style – Moderate Paced & Task Oriented

Conscientiousness style individuals are detail oriented people who enjoy working on complex projects and usually have superior technical knowledge (compared to the other three styles). In the workplace, this style's priority is to do an excellent job—as the name suggests, they are very conscientious. Socializing with co-workers is of lowest priority…and at times, they can come across as anti-social due to their high focus on work and unwillingness to socialize with anyone during work hours. Team members with high social needs—such as I or S-style individuals—will often feel uncomfortable around the introvert C-style; and the C-style will feel stressed around individuals who constantly try to distract them with non-work related conversations.

C-style individuals are usually very diplomatic and polite but can come across as a bit distant. They'll treat everyone with respect, but if they feel disrespected or pressured, they can retort by becoming overly introverted and non-communicative, withholding critical information, communicating with co-workers in terms that are above their competence levels, or otherwise sabotage workflow.

The challenge with both S-style and C-style individuals is that they tend to avoid verbalizing their hurt or frustration. You can offend them without even realizing it, and they will not express their hurt feelings to you. While the S-style might let you know after a few weeks or months about what you did (especially if you do it repeatedly), the C-style might carry around a grudge for years (or forever) without ever letting you know about it. But, you may feel that something is off when he or she communicates with you—with standoffish body language and use of very short, cold communication, for example. In other words, rather than blatantly telling you something is wrong, a C-style individual will give you the "cold treatment" to get even with you.

Here are some tips that will help you stay in good terms with the Conscientiousness style coworker:

1. Speak in short sentences, stick to facts, and stay away from jokes and stories.

2. Don't try to "wing it" when talking to this style—they can get frustrated and annoyed when someone is wasting their time with what they perceive as "nonsense" chat. Instead, ask for help—they love to talk about work related technical stuff.

3. Don't criticize their work. They usually put in hours, weeks, or months of thought and hard work into whatever they do, and do not take it lightly when someone just walks up and questions the accuracy of their production or efforts. If you do think there's a glitch in their output, make sure you can back up your claim with numbers, logic, and facts. Instead of criticizing, ask open ended questions about the area where you see a problem (e.g., "John, all this looks super great, but I'm a bit puzzled on how 7 + 3 adds up to 11 on this line. Am I reading this the wrong way?").

4. Express your appreciation for their detailed and accurate work. This style is probably the most knowledgeable style on your team, but due to their often introverted nature, few people praise them. Be the one who notices and shows appreciation for their hard work.

5. If your subordinate is a C-style individual, make sure to provide clear deadlines. They want to do an excellent—or even perfect—job, and if left to work at their pace, they'll often take too much time to complete whatever they are working on.

C-style individuals are some of the hardest working and most knowledgeable individuals who come to work committed to do an excellent job.

As we discussed early on in the book, and as you may have gathered as you read the information about each style above, the opposite styles seem to have nothing in common. Understanding differences is crucial in order to create a harmonious and productive working relationships.

#16: Learn about and practice resilience and optimism

Some people are just born resilient. They seem to be able to handle stress, life-changing events, the death of a loved one, serious illness, traumatic accidents, and any other event life throws their way. The good news is that those of us who aren't as inherently resilient can learn to be.

According to the American Psychological Association (APA), "resilience is the process of adapting well in the face of adversity, trauma, tragedy, threats, or even significant sources of stress—such as family and relationship problems, serious health problems, or workplace and financial stressors. It means 'bouncing back' from difficult experiences." Being resilient does not mean that a person doesn't experience stress at all, or in this case, that a bully won't hurt their feelings or cause them to get stressed out or even depressed. What it does mean, however, is that people who are resilient are better at getting over these upsetting feelings and moving forward, rather than dwelling on the bullying and allowing it to engulf their life.

Researchers who have focused on resilience have found that people who are resilient have:

- A support system of friends and caring people both in and outside of their family
- The capacity to make realistic plans to overcome their trauma, and to see those plans through
- A positive view of themselves
- Effective communication skills
- The ability to maintain control of their feelings.

With that said, there are several things you can do to build up your own resilience. This chapter encompasses many of them already, including encouraging you to seek support from friends and family, and report your problem to management. We've also offered tools to help you keep things in perspective and to help you with your communication skills.

To reiterate some of these ideas in the context of resilience, it is important to avoid seeing this problem with bullying as something that you will never be able to overcome. You can't change the bully, but you can change how you respond to him or her. That's what you have control over. Try looking beyond what's happening now and focus on your better future, because your future is something you have control over.

The next step, then, is to make plans for that new and brighter future, and then take decisive actions to make them happen. As they say, "A goal without a plan is just a wish." You have to set a goal for rectifying your situation, make a plan, and then take action to make the goal come to fruition. Even if the actions you take are small from day to day, they still bring you one step closer to your brighter future. If your goal is to find a new job, for example, you don't have to quit your current job tomorrow. But you do have to get started on your resume, look at a job posting or two online, or send an email out to your friends to let them know that you are looking for something new. Even on days when taking action seems impossible because of your mood or your schedule, ask yourself, "What's one small thing I can do today that will help me achieve my goal?" We encourage you to do at least one thing to reach your goal each and every day.

You must also remain optimistic to maintain your resilience. This is a hard one when you're getting beaten down day in and day out by a bully, there's no question. But you can do it. In order to do so, you will have to make a cognizant effort to remain positive. Luckily, the spiral effect is on your side.

Researchers have found that we easily fall into a spiral effect—but whether it's a positive or negative one is up to you. In other words, every time you make a negative comment to yourself, the chances that you will make another negative comment go up exponentially. Then you make another negative comment to yourself, and then another, and another. Soon you're in a downward spiral of negativity. But if you break that cycle, and tell yourself one positive thing, and then another, and another, soon you're in an upward spiral of positivity. You just have to make that effort to be positive to get the spiral going in the right direction.

To be honest, studying resilience has been an extremely powerful and therapeutic tool for one of the authors, who became an expert on bullying because of her own experiences being bullied. Rather than trying to figure out why she'd been victimized, she spent a lot of time understanding how to become stronger. She avoided being a victim, and made the choice to control her own destiny. Then, recently, she was in a terrible accident and wound up in the hospital for several days with many broken bones and a skull that was essentially pulverized. She had one eye sewn shut, her jaw wired closed and a cast on both arms. Despite many odds and being told that she would not return to work for several months, within less than 30 days she was in front of a college classroom, teaching. This was possible because of positive thinking and resilience – tools she picked up along the way in studying workplace bullying. She made the choice not be a victim of circumstance, but a courageous individual who could overcome the odds.

If you think you can't get through this situation with the bully, you're wrong. You can, and you will. There are many books, tools and resources out there for building up your own wall of resilience, and we encourage you to seek them out.

#17: See a doctor and keep documentation regarding your health

If you decide to see a specialist due to the workplace stress, share your workplace experiences with your doctor or therapist. Bring this book and other materials you have collected with you to the appointment in order to give your doctor a complete picture of what you are experiencing at work. If the final diagnosis is a stress-related disorder, depression, or anxiety, seek documentation from them that the bullying you experienced at work was the cause of your ailment. (You also might need this documentation later for workers' compensation, leave from work, or should you find yourself in court.)

#18: Enlist support from friends, family, superiors, and co-workers

Having people to talk to—whether at work or at home—can make all the difference in the world. Often verbalizing your feelings can help you see things more clearly. Talk to your support system about what's happening so that they know why you are feeling upset or depressed. They can provide support and guidance as you work your way through the maze of options for getting out of this situation successfully. If you need to, ask them to read this book and other materials you have collected on the topic so that they have a true understanding of how much pain you are in. Tell them exactly how you are feeling, and tell them you need their support.

Caution! It is extremely important that you don't ask co-workers to take sides. Simply let them know what's going on and how it affects your work. In the eyes of management, if you have been attempting to turn people against the bully by asking them to take sides, you will look just as unprofessional as the person doing the bullying. Seeking support from co-workers and superiors is different from asking them to turn against the bully; be sure you're not doing the latter.

As you seek support from co-workers, ask them if they notice whether a certain individual is a little too aggressive or unprofessional. If they say no, they don't really see any problems with anyone's behavior, then drop it and walk away. Do not try to convince them otherwise. If they say yes, they indeed noticed bullying, ask a few questions to gain some facts about what they've witnessed. Do not let the conversation turn into a venting session, and do not bad mouth the bully by calling him or her names. You never know whose side they are really on, and because it is important that you remain as professional as possible, you've got to be careful about the way you talk about others at work. Just find out where your co-worker stands. If he or she will let you, provide their name when you file your grievance or make a report, or ask if they will come with you to make it. There's power in numbers, and the more people who complain the more likely it is that management will believe you. If your co-worker declines, let it go, do not beg them to join forces or do something they don't want to do.

#19: Stay away from social media

If you have a social media page such as Facebook, Twitter, or LinkedIn, it is important to keep information about your bullying situation at work off of your profile page or any other online

Seeking support

Do not ask your co-workers to take sides. You can ask them for their encouragement, and you can ask them if they'd be willing to be listed as a witness to some of the abuse in your report to management, but you cannot ask them to take your side. Of course, your family and friends *are* on your side.

Asking co-workers to take sides is unprofessional and can hurt you in the long run, particularly if it gets back to the person bullying you.

media. While it might be tempting to post status updates about how much of a jerk your boss was today, it is ill-advised to do so. Not only can this be a shortcut to losing your job, but this is also likely to hinder you from getting jobs in the future.

In the next chapter, we will discuss how to make a successful report to management. Your objective right now—as hard as this might seem—is to remain calm, cool, collected, and very professional. Understand that your social media page and anything else you post on the Internet is in the public domain. If you make a complaint about a bullying co-worker, and your boss looks at your social media page only to find that you've been openly posting comments about the bully online, your credibility is shot. Your complaint might be out the window.

Please also note that just because your page is set to "friends only" or "private" you should never assume that to be the reality. Facebook, for example, has taken the liberty of changing privacy settings automatically when they've updated their website, a problem for many people who later lost their jobs because of it. So again, keep comments about the bully, the situation, or your feelings about it off-line.

#20: Take care of you

Because of the toll bullying can take on you, it is is very important that you are aware of your mental and physical state and you do what's needed to be sure that you are safe and happy.

You are the most important person in the world—so take care of yourself. If you need to call in sick because you're feeling like you can't go to work today, then do it. If you need to see a doctor or therapist to help you through what's happening, then do it. If you need to quit your job because you've tried everything and nothing's working, then do it.

#21: Open your mind to new opportunities

There's no job in the world that's worth the loss of your sanity, self-respect, and dignity. If you tried everything, but things are still not getting better, then quit—take your strength to another company where you'll be appreciated. Nothing is worth losing your health over. You can always get another job, but once you lose your health it's not so simple to regain it.

Yes, it's true, finding a new job it's not always easy, but trying to heal from the severe damages of bullying can take years. Some have even given their life, rather than find a new job. Please don't let it come to that for you.

In order to break your ties and leave the organization, you first have to realize just how much of your identity, or who you are as a person, is wrapped up in your job or career. We spend 8, 10, 12 hours a day at work, so it's natural that we would rely on our position and job responsibilities for self-esteem and identity. But when there's workplace bullying, your identity morphs into one of being a victim who goes to work every day to a place that makes you feel miserable. You only have one life to live—so why not live it in peace.

The fact of the matter is that targets often do not receive the help they are looking for when they *do* report their situations to their managers or human resources. In the next chapter, we'll discuss everything you need to do to prepare to make that report to your managers. If you don't report it, there's no chance your situation will get better. If you do report it, there's no guarantee your managers will help you. But, if you report it, and they don't help, at least your conscience is clear knowing that you've tried; and if nothing improves it's time to move on to an organization that values your contributions and your well-being. This leads us into the next item: how to tiptoe around the bullying issue during a job interview with a new prospective employer.

#22: Prepare for job interviews

The first thing you want to do to get prepared for an interview is create a strengths inventory. This is a list of things you are good at and assets you bring to the table. Your inventory should include a strength, and then an representation of that strength. For example, you might write that you are great at working productively under pressure, and then you should jot down some notes about a few times when you did indeed work productively under pressure. You are a much stronger candidate for any job if you can provide real, behavior-based examples of your strengths.

Strengths inventory

Before an interview, take an "inventory" of your strengths.

Ex: Great at resolving customer complaints. Received 2 awards for customer service.

_____

_____

_____

_____

_____

_____

_____

_____

_____

_____

Keep in mind that interviewers are always looking for a few important characteristics, no matter what position and no matter what industry. They are as follows:

- You can demonstrate you have initiative and company loyalty
- You are solution-oriented and forward thinking (that means when you have a problem, you attempt to find a solution before bringing the problem to your manager)
- You have a long list of accomplishments, rather than job tasks, to share during the interview and on your resume
- You can work in a team.

During the entire interview, you should be focusing on these four things. Every answer you give should provide proof that you hold these credentials. This is important because if you can prove you have initiative, are solution-oriented, are goal oriented (can achieve things), and can work in a team, what happened at your last employer won't really matter to the prospective employer because you'll make a good-looking candidate.

Now comes the part during the interview where they ask about why you left your previous employer. There are a few ways you can handle it.

The first is to simply say that you weren't receiving growth opportunities and needed to move on. This is not a very informative answer and may lead to more probing from the interviewer. It could also communicate that you are hiding something or holding back. Not good.

The second option is to provide some other reason un-related to the bully. This could work, but could also be unethical and therefore not a desired response either.

The third choice is a bit more intricate, but it demonstrates you meet the four universal criteria for a potential employee, and above all shows that you are honest. Here's an example of how you might answer the question, "Can you tell me why you left your previous organization?"

> *I am a go-getter. I really like opportunities to do new projects and learn new things, and unfortunately my previous employer wasn't offering those types of opportunities to me anymore* (demonstrates initiative).

For example, during my first year at the organization, I developed a new procedure for handling, documenting, and tracking customer complaints; conceived and was responsible for the internal company newsletter; and created and managed a file clerk position (demonstrates accomplishments). *After awhile, however, these opportunities to contribute positively to the organization seemed to get taken away by one manager in particular.*

I really believe I put effort into directly resolving my differences with this manager. I enjoyed my job and working for the company, and of course I wanted to be sure I was getting along with my manager (demonstrates you are a team player). *When talking with the manager about our relationship didn't seem to work, I spoke to the company owners about it* (demonstrates initiative and that you are solution-oriented). *I suggested to them that I move teams so our relationship didn't get in the way of production and customer service* (demonstrates company loyalty).

Unfortunately, the owners didn't seem to think this person's behavior was all that bad and only put her on warning for her behavior once I'd left the company. But, ultimately, while I got along with everyone else at the organization (demonstrates you are a team player), *this particular individual really made working for that organization difficult, and I decided leaving was my best option.*

In my current job search, I am really looking for an organization that appreciates and even praises initiative and hard work, because those are two of my best qualities (demonstrates initiative).

There are a few other things we'd like to add here.

It is always a good idea to avoid bad-mouthing your previous employer. Your response to the question about why you left must be polite, eloquent, and honest. Talk around any negative feelings you have about the company and the bully—the new employer doesn't need to hear it. And, they'll wonder what will happen if they rub you the wrong way and you leave—are you going to bad mouth them, too?

Always make a point of building rapport with the interviewer from the time you meet and shake hands. The interview should flow more like a conversation than an interview, and if it does, then you know you have built rapport. You can do this by being relaxed and conversational, and by asking the interviewer questions about themselves. If you spot a picture on his or her desk from Lake Tahoe, for example, mention that you've always wanted to go there and ask him or her how the trip was.

Also, mirror the interviewer's body language slightly. This builds a subconscious liking for you because you seem similar to the interviewer—something we look for in everyone we meet. If he takes a sip of water, you take a sip of water. If she crosses her legs, you cross yours. Don't be a copy cat, but follow along every once in a while.

If you build rapport with interviewers, then they will find you to be a positive person that they like, and one that couldn't possibly be responsible for what happened at the last company.

Further, there are questions you can ask during the interview process to ensure you won't wind up working with another bully. Business and financial guru, Guy Kawasaki, wrote a blog post about this (2007) with the help of Bob Sutton, author of the book,

The No Asshole Rule: Building a Civilized Workplace and Surviving One That Isn't. With their blessing, we have "re-printed" the questions:

1. **Kisses-up and kicks-down**: "How does the prospective boss respond to feedback from people higher in rank and lower in rank?" "Can you provide examples from experience?" One characteristic of certified assholes is that they tend to demean those who are less powerful while brown-nosing their superiors.

2. **Can't take it**: "Does the prospective boss accept criticism or blame when the going gets tough?" Be wary of people who constantly dish out criticism but can't take a healthy dose themselves.

3. **Short fuse**: "In what situations have you seen the prospective boss lose his temper?" Sometimes anger is justified or even effective when used sparingly, but someone who "shoots-the-messenger" too often can breed a climate of fear in the workplace. Are co-workers scared of getting in an elevator with this person?

4. **Bad credit**: "Which style best describes the prospective boss: gives out gratuitous credit, assigns credit where credit is due, or believes everyone should be their own champion?" This question opens the door to discuss whether or not someone tends to take a lot of credit while not recognizing the work of his or her team.

5. **Canker sore**: "What do past collaborators say about working with the prospective boss?" Assholes usually have a history of infecting teams with nasty and dysfunctional conflict. The world seems willing to tolerate talented assholes, but that doesn't mean you have to.

6. **Flamer:** What kind of email sender is the prospective boss? Most assholes cannot contain themselves when it

comes to email: flaming people, carbon-copying the world, blind carbon copying to cover his own buttocks. Email etiquette is a window into one's soul.

7. **Downer**: "What types of people find it difficult to work with the prospective boss? What type of people seem to work very well with the prospective boss?" Pay attention to responses that suggest "strong-willed" or "self-motivated" people tend to work best with the prospective boss because assholes tend to leave people around them feeling de-energized and deflated.

8. **Card shark**: "Does the prospective boss share information for everyone's benefit?" A tendency to hold cards close to one's chest—i.e., a reluctance to share information—is a sign that this person treats co-workers as competitors who must be defeated so he or she can get ahead.

9. **Army of one**: "Would people pick the prospective boss for their team?" Sometimes there is upside to having an asshole on your team, but that won't matter if the coworkers refuse to work with that person. Use this question to help determine if the benefit of having the prospective boss on your team outweighs any asshole behaviors.

10. **Open architecture**: "How would the prospective boss respond if a copy of *The No Asshole Rule* appeared on her desk?" Be careful if the answer is, "Duck!"

In addition to avoiding a bullying boss, Kathryn Britton, author of the book, *Smarts and Stamina*, provides a list of questions you might consider asking to avoid a bullying workplace culture altogether. These questions are posted on her blog on the website, Positive Psychology News Daily (2009). She suggests asking:

1. Who will I learn from, and how will I learn it?

2. Who is considered a hero here? Why?

3. How is conflict resolved here?

4. How willing are people to help each other? Is helping others valued and expected? How much flexibility is there in divvying up work tasks?

5. A lot of organizations focus on what's not working; how do you celebrate what is working?

6. What keeps you going when things are stressful? Is it a sense of purpose or fear? Is this workplace made up of competition or comradeship?

#23: Take legal action

(This section contributed by Patricia G. Barnes, author of the blog: http://abusergoestowork.com. We thought it best you hear it from an attorney, though nothing here should be construed as legal advice.)

Several factors may compel you to consult an attorney to explore legal options. Since 2003, twenty states have considered adopting workplace anti-bully legislation that would give targets of workplace bullying a civil right to sue the bully and/or the employer for creating a "hostile work environment." As of the summer of 2011, however, no state has approved such a measure. The United States lags behind other industrialized countries that have passed laws and regulations to curb workplace bullying, including the United Kingdom, Canada, France, Ireland, Spain, and Sweden. In Victoria, Australia, workplace bullying is a crime!

Federal laws prohibit discrimination on the basis of age, disability, national origin, genetic information, pregnancy, race/color, religion, and sex. In addition, many states have adopted state laws that prohibit discrimination against gays and lesbians. These laws offer possible redress to targets of workplace bullying in the

United States who are members of a protected class. For example, bullying that includes inappropriate sexual conduct may constitute sexual harassment in violation of Title VII of the Civil Rights Act of 1964. Generally, targets must prove they were subjected to an intimidating, hostile, or offensive working environment. The U.S. Supreme Court has made it clear that Title VII is not intended to be a general civility code for the workplace; a plaintiff must show the harassment was due to the plaintiff's protected status. Unfortunately, targets of bullying who lack protected status are left with a hodgepodge of often ill-fitting legal remedies.

Most targets of workplace bullying end up quitting or are fired. If bullying becomes so intolerable that you are at the point of quitting, consider that you may be eligible for up to twelve weeks of leave under the Family and Medical Leave Act, 29 U.S.C. 2615, if you can show the bullying caused you to suffer a serious health condition that makes you unable to perform the essential functions of your job. If you have no choice but to quit, remember that you may still be eligible for unemployment benefits under the theory of constructive dismissal, which holds that the employer changed the fundamental terms and conditions of the job for which the employee was hired, effectively dismissing the employee.

Employees who are fired may be able to sue for breach of contract or wrongful termination if they have an employment contract, there is an anti-bullying policy in their employee handbook, or they are covered by a collective bargaining agreement. Most states adhere, at least to some degree, to the "employment at will" doctrine, which permits an employer to fire an employee for any reason that is not illegal (i.e., discrimination) or in violation of public policy (i.e., whistleblower). Possible tort actions include Intentional Infliction of Emotional Distress, Tortuous Interference with the Employment Relationship, defamation, invasion of privacy, and assault.

The Indiana Supreme Court, in a landmark bullying case, *Raess v. Doescher*, 883 N.E.2d 790 (2008), upheld an assault award of $325,000 to a hospital operating room technician, Joseph Doescher, who claimed he reasonably feared imminent harm from a cardiovascular surgeon, Daniel Raess. According to Doescher, Raess was angry because Doescher complained to hospital administrators of Raess' alleged bullying of other technicians. Raess "aggressively and rapidly advanced on the plaintiff with clenched fists, piercing eyes, beet-red face, popping veins, and screaming and swearing at him." Doescher backed up against a wall and put his hands up, believing that Raess was going to hit him. The doctor then "stormed past the plaintiff and left the room, momentarily stopping to declare to the plaintiff 'you're finished, you're history.'"

The tort of Intentional Infliction of Emotional Distress (IIED) would seem to be a promising claim for targets of workplace bullying because it provides damages for "extreme and outrageous conduct" that "intentionally or recklessly causes severe emotional distress to another." The Texas Supreme Court in 1999 affirmed an IIED award of $275,000 to three workers whose supervisor repeatedly shouted profanities at them, physically charged them, pounded his fists and threatened them with termination during a two-year period (*GTE Southwest, Inc. v. Bruce*, 998 S.W.2d 605, 613-14 [Tex. 1999]). However, many courts have found the conduct associated with workplace bullying to be insufficiently "extreme and outrageous" for IIED. This may change as society becomes more aware of the insidious and harmful nature of workplace bullying.

Many hurdles await targets of bullying who pursue legal options, not the least of which is finding an attorney who will take your case. However, even the threat of a lawsuit could encourage your employer to do what all American employers are technically already required by law to do. The Occupational Safety and Health Act, General Duty Clause, Section 5(a)(1) SEC. 5, states that all employers "shall furnish to each of his employees employment and a place of employment which are free from recognized hazards that are causing or are likely to cause death or serious physical harm to his employees … ." As you know, there is overwhelming research that workplace bullying can cause severe mental and physical harm to employees. So much so that in May 2011, the Occupational Safety and Health Administration (OSHA) adopted a safety program for its own workers that includes a workplace anti-bully policy.

CHAPTER 6: GETTING MANAGEMENT'S ATTENTION, AND HELP

Four types of manager reactions to bullying complaints, Seven must-do's before filing a grievance & Seven solutions to offer your managers

Reporting bullying behaviors to your manager or human resources department has probably crossed your mind, if you haven't done so already. Before we provide you with information that can help you make a report to management that will be successful, we want to make sure you have a full understanding of the possible consequences reporting bullying might have for you.

It is unfortunate that we have to address this at all. It makes sense that if a person complains to their manager about another person's abusive behavior, the manager's reaction would be to look into it and address it. But that's just not the reality many targets of bullying experience.

In the business world, the concept of workplace bullying is a lot like the concept of sexual harassment was in the '70s and early '80s. Although laws against sexual harassment were passed with Title VII of the Civil Rights Act of 1964, it wasn't until 1986 that a case regarding sexual harassment was heard by the Supreme Court. Until then, many companies failed to properly address it, develop policies against it, or take actions against perpetrators even though the law said they should. Only after sexual harassment received a large amount of press in 1991, with the case of Anita Hill versus Supreme Court nominee Clarence Thomas, did organizations take serious note of the issue. Until workplace bullying receives more press, and until it becomes illegal in the

United States, complaints share the same doom sexual harassment complaints did prior to 1991.

All that said, be advised that managers, supervisors, company owners, and human resources representatives (hereafter we will refer to these groups collectively as "managers") will display one of four reactions to a report of workplace bullying. You will not know which reaction you will get until you file your complaint, so it is important to be aware of the four possibilities. Or, perhaps you have heard rumors around your company regarding complaints that have been made in the past and management's reaction to them, and this can serve as useful information too.

#1: The empathetic manager

The first, most uncommon, yet most desirable reaction is one of engagement and empathy. Indeed, we have heard several stories from individuals who reported bullying to their managers and in response the complaint was investigated, and the bullying was addressed and the bully even disciplined. Obviously, this is the most ideal scenario.

#2: The well-meaning manager

The second type of reaction from managers is one of compassion, but because of being uninformed or uneducated in the concept of workplace bullying, the wrong action is taken. Many managers don't necessarily believe adults bully other adults, but will listen with empathy as targets describe their situation. They want to help resolve the problem but unfortunately, these managers often take the wrong action—a result of not having a full understanding of workplace bullying. These managers may determine that the bully and target should go through mediation to resolve their differences, that one or both parties should receive conflict management training, or that the target should be transferred to another department to get away from the bully. These managers may also choose not to take any action because they believe the issue is an interpersonal conflict rather than bullying, and that the target should work it out on his or her own.

#3: The indifferent manager

While the well-meaning manager does feel empathy for your situation, the indifferent manager simply disagrees that bullying is a problem, or doesn't hear anything in your grievance that constitutes action on their part. Indifferent managers will simply turn you away with instructions to deal with the problem on your own.

#4: The cynical manager

The fourth, most popular yet most undesirable manager reaction is one of cynicism. These managers are absolutely convinced that there is no way bullying exists. Beyond that, these managers also believe that targets who complain of bullying are actually poor performers who can't take the criticism. These managers think targets are at fault, that they need to grow thicker skin, and that they need to quickly adjust their performance and their attitude in order to keep their job.

Examples of these types of managers were evident in an online forum in which one of the authors participated. Comments from these managers included:

> *"There seems to be a growing trend that every time someone's boss yells at them it's a workplace conflict that also suggests the boss is a bully. That may occasionally be true, but more often than not, in over thirty years of workplace experience, I*

have observed it is an under-producing or non-producing employee (filing the complaint)."

"Honestly, I read a lot of posts on a different forum that is open to the public and has a lot of employees posting their situations about bosses bullying employees and 99% of them are such that I can see by their posts what the issue is—low performance, too much time off, their attitude in the postings, etc. In my twenty-year career, I can honestly tell you that I have seen only one bully boss. Out of hundreds...."

"There are those that think they are bullied because the employer expects them to be at work on time consistently. Because the employer doesn't take all the excuses for missed work and productivity. Or they take exasperation and criticism as bullying."

During this online conversation within the forum, the managers were asked why they were so opposed to the idea that workplace bullying exists. Answers included:

"I was in HR when the diversity fad developed, and suddenly every fringe consultant was an expert in diversity and offering their services to help implement diversity programs. They were aggressive—if you didn't have a diversity program, then somehow your company was uncaring, insensitive, even Neanderthal in your approach to business. Diversity programs have yet to produce any measurable benefit, yet businesses spent huge amounts of money on it."

"So it goes with HR fads—it seems like HR is plagued with them every five years or so. Some get a lot of publicity, like diversity, others don't. All fade into oblivion, some mercifully sooner rather than later."

> *"HR has seen a bunch of fads. I would agree bullying is but one more."*

We are sharing all of this with you because we want you to have a full understanding of what the potential outcome of talking with your managers might be. Every circumstance is different, and no one can guess what action your managers or HR department will take. And because of the possibility that your manager might have one of the more uncaring attitudes we described above, we want to provide you with the tools you need to prepare to make your report or file a formal grievance.

This chapter will attempt to provide everything you need to do to prepare yourself before you make that appointment with your manager to file a grievance. In addition, because most managers would prefer that you provide a solution along with your complaint, we will provide solutions you might consider offering your managers.

Seven must-do's before you file a grievance

We recommend using the following guide to prepare for reporting your situation to managers or HR. Gathering your thoughts and this information will help you focus your conversation. Bring your answers with you, as they will be a helpful reminder of what you need to accomplish. The more you are able to stay in control, and be clear and helpful, the more things will pan out in your favor.

The questions we ask below and the tasks we have provided for you to do may seem a bit overwhelming, particularly if you have been getting bullied at work for a long time or the behaviors have become so severe that you are bordering—or reached—a state of depression. Please understand that the conversation will go much better for you if you are prepared. If you find these questions are taking a toll on you as you attempt to answer them, just do the best you can.

We have provided a worksheet in Appendix A to help. As you read the rest of this chapter, use the worksheet to assist you in gathering up the right documentation and getting into the right state of mind to make your complaint.

#1: Document the workplace bullying

The first, and perhaps the most important thing you must do to prepare for making a report, is document the damaging behaviors. Even if you think you'll never make a complaint, if you're being bullied you should be proactive and document your experiences. You just never know when the information might be useful.

Document all incidents in a journal of some kind. Be sure to record the following information every time a bullying incident occurs:

- **Who:** the name of the perpetrator, any witnesses who saw the bullying happen
- **What:** behaviors you saw or were the target of, what was said
- **When:** dates when the behaviors occurred
- **Where:** location and the event (e.g., staff meeting, inside a person's office during debrief)
- **Supporting documents:** what documents, if any, can you provide with regard to this incident

It is important to remember, as you fill out this journal, that you must stick to the facts. We will say that again because it is so important: stick to the facts and facts only. Avoid writing about your emotions as much as possible.

In fact, we suggest that you purchase two journals for yourself; use one to document bullying behaviors when they occur and use the second to write about your emotions. The journal you keep the facts in will be one that you may potentially provide to management, while the journal you write your emotions in will be one that stays at home and is never shared with anyone at work. (By the way, writing down your emotions is a healthy exercise. It will help you tremendously in clarifying your emotions and can help you vent and unload your feelings.)

It is so vitally imperative that you only write down the facts because facts are what your manager will respond to. Although managers should care about whether employees get along and whether your feelings are hurt, feelings aren't related to the bottom line and therefore are somewhat irrelevant from the manager's perspective. In the words of a thirty-year HR veteran in that online forum:

> *"Unfortunately HR and management usually do NOT have the ability to go 'personal' with employees. To dig deep into the reasons and feelings and emotions. To smooth over hurt feelings. To babysit one who is feeling persecuted. At some point, it DOES need to get back to the business of running the company and working towards that goal and needs to be less about feelings and more about realistic expectations and being productive and putting personal feelings/perspectives aside."*

In other words, targets who provide information to their managers about how they feel about the bullying are the targets who are seen as whiney low performers who need to adjust their attitude. So stick to the facts. Any and every time you experience or witness a bullying behavior, get to your desk immediately and jot down everything you can remember. Write down as many details as you can, and focus only on describing the bullying behaviors in detail—not on how you felt about them.

It is also highly recommended that you collect any documents you can that support your claim. Possible documents include:

- Memos, emails, and other tangible items you have on file to prove the behavior (e.g., intentional misleading instructions, foul language, etc.)
- Lists of witnesses and people who have seen the behavior occurring and who told you they would be okay with you including their name in your report
- Written testimonials from witnesses if they are willing to write them
- Your personnel records
- Your performance reports
- Applicable company policies that were violated
- Incident reports
- Applicable contracts
- Physical and mental health documents, bills, and payments from doctors
- Calendar of incidents, meetings, or other events where bullying occurred
- Relevant meeting notes
- This book, as well as research articles by experts that prove your concerns about employee performance are valid
- Anything else that may serve as proof or supporting data—when in doubt, include it

On a final note regarding documentation, we want to make sure you understand that anything on your work computer or on your work phone or voicemail belongs to your employer. Your employer has the right to search through your company email, listen to your voicemails, and search anything else that belongs to them. It is very important, then, that as you are keeping your journal and collecting documentation that you avoid doing so on your computer.

It may seem old-fashioned to actually write things down in a journal, but it's the only way to ensure that the information in it remains private until you're ready to share it. The last thing you need is your bullying boss to crack into your computer or your email account and find a folder of electronic journal entries about him or her. The only way to keep it safe is to keep it with you, and take it home with you at night or lock it in a drawer to which only you have the key. Alternatively, if you have a personal laptop that you carry to work, keep your records there in a password-protected document.

#2: Seek confirmation that you are a good employee and high-performer

If the bully hasn't already called your performance into question through performance evaluations, he or she will once they find out you've talked to management. For this reason, it is strongly suggested that you collect data that supports that you are a high-performer. Talk to other employees you work with, perhaps a former supervisor in a different department, or even a few customers if you can to ensure that others believe you are a strong performer and will tell your manager.

Think about this from a manager's point of view. If an employee makes a complaint about their supervisor, for example, and the employee is late all of the time, rarely makes quota, and is often caught chatting instead of working, is the manager going to take immediate action against the supervisor? Probably not. If the employee is always on time, always beats quota, and is often found working hard and not socializing, the complaint the employee makes against the supervisor has much more validity. So be sure you are the latter. Be sure you are someone who's words will be trusted.

Workplace bullying will indeed take down your self-esteem and thwart your self-concept. In turn, your performance will suffer, and it is very likely you will find yourself calling in sick more often than you ever did before you were bullied. Do your absolute best to avoid any behavior that can be called low performance by anyone. Remain strong, stay focused on your tasks, do your work, and do it well. Be the best that you can be at all times. Don't give the bully any leverage.

#3: Address poor performance evaluations

The previous tip leads to an important suggestion for dealing with a manager who is a workplace bully. If the bully is your manager, and he or she did use a performance evaluation to bully you, it is important that you take certain steps in order to address this issue with your manager first before filing a grievance with the higher-ups.

Effective performance evaluations are positive and ongoing, provide constructive feedback, and offer specific goals for you to complete. A manager who knows how to deliver evaluations will meet with you no less than once per quarter, and during the meeting will provide a list of all of the things you are doing right, and some insight into areas upon which they would like to see you improve. As they discuss those areas, they will also work with you to develop goals to ensure that you do indeed have the opportunity to improve.

For example, if you are not making the quota for customer service calls, a bad manager will just write that down in your evaluation and leave it at that. A good manager will ask you why you think you aren't meeting the quota, and set incremental goals for you, as well as work with you to ensure you have the resources you need to meet them. The manager will say, then, "Let's set a goal for you to increase call volume by 10% within the next two weeks, and by 20% by the end of the month. I will check in with you every few days to ensure you are on your way to meeting them. I'm also going to assign one of our top call center reps to work with you on training, and he will ensure you have what you need to make your calls successful. We will re-visit this in a month, and if you haven't improved by then, then we will need to talk about what our next steps should be."

Effective Performance Evaluations

Effective performance evaluations will have the following items:

- What you are doing well
- What you can improve upon in specific terms, and:
    - Quantifiable goals to improve
    - When the goals should be completed
    - How reaching the goals will be measured
    - What resources will be provided to help you to reach the goals
    - How often your manager will check in to gauge progress
    - What will happen if the goals are not met

If your performance evaluation is more like the former, and you only receive a note in your file that you are not meeting quota, but no other information or resources are provided, then you have a problem. You should send an email to your boss requesting a meeting to discuss your evaluation. Send an email so you will have proof of your request for information and proof of their response. If your request is ignored, send a few more and now you have proof that you tried to obtain guidance and improve your performance. If your request is accepted, set a meeting date and request that the following be addressed during the meeting:

- What exact behaviors need to improve
- What specific goals you can set to improve your performance
- By when the goals you set need to be accomplished
- What measure of success can you present to prove the goal was reached
- What resources will be provided to ensure you meet your goals
- What the consequences are if you do not meet them

Any manager that does not provide this information to you is not performing their own managerial duties correctly. If the manager refuses to provide this information to you, they are setting you up for failure whether they mean to or not. If the manager does not provide this information to you, and you make a complaint about their bullying behaviors and your performance is called into question, now you have proof that you tried to improve.

Please note that if poor performance evaluations are the only bullying behavior you experience, then this is not bullying. Many managers struggle with the ability to deliver effective and positive performance evaluations, and many managers have different views on what type of performance is a good performance. In many cases, employees have long since received good employee reviews from one manager, and when they find themselves reporting to someone else all of a sudden they have poor performance reviews. This is a simple case of new management or differing ideas on your performance. Remember that bullying must be ongoing and involves a variety of behaviors to be considered bullying.

#4: Determine costs to the organization

Management and HR speaks the language of business: money. The saying "money talks" is no BS.

Therefore, presenting your case in factual, tangible terms will be to your benefit. We recommend you start by asking and answering the following types of questions:

- How much money has the bullying cost the organization?
- Have you witnessed him or her yelling at customers?
- Have you seen another employee underperform or quit as a result of the behavior?
- How much time do others spend gossiping about events transpiring around the bully's outbursts?
- Does it seem like morale in your department is declining? How do you know?
- Have some employees, including yourself, taken days off to avoid working with the bully?
- Have you or others seen a doctor during work hours to deal with stress, ulcers, or other ailments as a result of the bullying?

> **From the book, *One Minute Manager***
>
> *"...I do not want to hear about only attitudes or feelings. Tell me what is happening in observable, measurable terms."*
>
> -Kenneth Blanchard, PhD & Spencer Johnson, MD

In the next chapter, we will give you a long list of ways bullies wreak havoc on the organization. Using your answers to the questions we've provided here, and the guidance we've provided in the next chapter, you should be able to come up with some actual costs and prove the bully is hurting the bottom line.

This is an example of what you might present to managers:

Description	Cost
Time spent by human resources hiring replacements for people who have left	$20,000
Time spent by five employees talking about the bullying behaviors exhibited in the staff meeting, after the staff meeting is over	$1,000
Overtime costs associated with high demands of bully that go beyond normal working requests	$15,000
Time spent by three employees not working at full capacity because they spend time worrying and talking about the bullying behaviors	$18,000
Cost of lost client because employee called in sick due to fear of dealing with abusive behaviors	$10,000
Cost of lost client who left because he was bullied	$25,000
Time spent by human resources dealing with appeals to unemployment insurance because of people who were fired at the hands of the bully	$5,000
Estimated total cost of the bully	**-$94,000**
Revenue earned by the bully	**$100,000**
Total actual revenue brought in by the bully	**$6,000**

5: Attempt to resolve the issue yourself

If you've already done research on workplace bullying prior to reading this book, then you know that many bullying experts disagree with this advice. Many experts will tell you that this is a bad move—that standing up for yourself will only make the bullying worse. In fact, research does seem to indicate that bullying gets worse when targets attempt to stand up for themselves, and that bullying gets worse if a complaint is made but management doesn't resolve it correctly. Bullies like it when you don't stand up for yourself; it makes it easier on them if you don't. It helps solidify their thoughts that you are someone who can be walked all over, and of course it just makes the process of bullying you less work. And, telling management is threatening behavior to your bully, so backlash may be imminent when management does not take corrective action.

However, from a manager's viewpoint—and if you are going to be successful in making a complaint—a target who has taken steps to resolve their own relational issues is more powerful and taken more seriously than one who has not. Consider the following scenarios from a manager's perspective, and decide which one you would prefer if you were a manager taking a complaint about bullying:

Scenario A:

Employee: *Can I talk to you for a minute? My manager and I are not getting along, and I was hoping you would be able to work with me.*

Manager: *Sure, what's going on?*

Employee: *Rick seems to pick on me pretty regularly. Yesterday, for example, he interrupted me with rude comments in the staff meeting while I was talking. His behavior was disrespectful and unprofessional. He also gave me a horrible employee evaluation for this quarter, but I've always gotten great evaluations so I'm not sure what's going on there. There were plenty of scenarios in* recent months where Rick has been pretty aggressive with me. These are just a few examples.

Manager: *Well, have you talked to him? I'm sure he doesn't mean anything by it.*

Employee: *No, not really. He makes me nervous so I haven't been able to talk to him.*

Scenario B:

Employee: *Can I talk to you for a minute? My manager and I are not getting along, and I was hoping you would be able to work with me.*

Manager: *Sure, what's going on?*

Employee: *Rick seems to pick on me pretty regularly. Yesterday, for example, he interrupted me with rude comments in the staff meeting while I was talking. His behavior was disrespectful and unprofessional. He also gave me a horrible employee evaluation for this quarter, but I've always gotten great evaluations so I'm not sure what's going on there. There were plenty of scenarios in recent months where Rick has been pretty aggressive with me. These are just a few examples.*

Manager: *Well, have you talked to him? I'm sure he doesn't mean anything by it.*

Employee: *Yes, I have. After the staff meeting yesterday I pulled him aside and asked him about the disrespectful behavior, and he just said that I was making it up and being dramatic. During the past few weeks, I also asked him in person as well as emailed him several times requesting a meeting where he could provide me with more information about my employee review so I could figure out how to improve, and he just ignored my emails. Here's a copy of the four emails I sent requesting a meeting with him, all of which were ignored. I can't improve if Rick won't give me feedback on what to do differently.*

I'm coming to you because I have tried to address Rick's behavior towards me with him, but he's just not willing to talk to me. When I approached him this morning, he yelled at me and told me not to bug him. I do have a few ideas about what I can do to rectify the situation, and I wanted to bounce them off of you and find out what you thought was the most appropriate course of action for me to take.

Any manager would prefer scenario B, in any situation whether it be about bullying, a problem with a customer, an issue with some software you're using, or anything else. Managers like to know that you have taken steps to resolve the issue on your own first, before you came to them. In scenario B, not only were we able to say that we'd already tried two of our own solutions, but that we had brainstormed several more and wanted to get feedback on them. From a manager's perspective, the employee in scenario B appears innovative, confident, and able to solve their own problems; while the employee in scenario A appears helpless, whining, and unable to work well with others.

In order to be the employee in scenario B, you will have to find a way to address the bullying at least two or three times before you go to your manager. Use the tools we provided in the last chapter regarding assertiveness, effective communication, and courage in order to make this happen. If you need to, bring a co-worker with you to sit in for moral support when talking to your bully.

The other benefit to attempting to resolve the issue yourself is that having these stories of courage will be valuable if you decide to seek other employment, as we discussed in the previous chapter.

#6: Get prepared for the conversation

Understand your goals and expected outcomes:

It is really important that you go into the conversation with pre-determined goals and outcomes. If you go in just to complain, you will be seen as a complainer. If you go in with specific action items in mind, you will be seen as an individual working toward making the workplace better. And for your own sanity, you must decide what end result you'd like out of your conversation with management. Spend some time deciding what the purpose of your talk is, and develop tangible, real goals that you are seeking. You've got to have more than, "I just want him to be nice to me." So think about why you are having this conversation. Ask yourself the following questions:

- What do you want to accomplish?
- Are you imparting information, alerting the organization to a situation they need to be aware of? Or are you trying to make the organization take action against your aggressor?
- Do you want them to transfer you to a new department?
- By what date should the organization take action?
- How will you know you've accomplished what you needed? How will you know the goals you set for the conversation were reached?
- What will you do if the goals you set are not reached? Which goals are you willing to give up?

Think about how you will communicate:

In addition to understanding your goals, we recommend you jot down some notes about how you would like to present yourself during the conversation, and why it is important to remain calm and collected. Preparing yourself in advance will help you to behave as you wish to behave instead of being overwhelmed by your own pain and fears. List the ways you want to "be" during the interaction in order for you to achieve your goal. (Ex. Neutral, calm, thoughtful, forthright, "centered.")

Get prepared to discuss the behaviors, not your feelings:

We cannot overemphasize the power of presenting facts over opinions. You need this manager or HR representative to advocate for you, and *the more you remain a reporter of facts instead of a target of someone's bad behavior, the greater the likelihood that you will succeed.* Simply put, you must avoid talking about you and how you feel, and focus on talking about the bully, his or her behaviors, and how they are causing damage to the organization. Avoid saying "I" as much as you can.

Should you use the term "bully" during your complaint?

The answer is yes. Although the word is a new term for many in the business world, the term "bully" is advised because it is relatable for your managers. Most people know what that term means.

However, consider using a variety of other adjectives, too. Using words like "verbally abusive," "overly aggressive," and "unprofessional" can help you make your case because they accurately describe what is happening.

The most important thing to remember, however, is that you must describe the individual's *behavior*. Do not call the individual names; use these terms to describe his or her *behavior*.

195

This is challenging because we have many strong feelings about our bullying experience. We feel fear, anger, disgust, anxiety, and despair mixed in with hope and vulnerability because we want our manager or HR representative to help us. But the person to whom you're reporting may be afraid of feelings and emotions, or they may not think that your feelings are a good enough reason to take action. Many of us don't know what to say when someone's upset, and from a business management perspective, your emotions are not causing damage to the bottom line—the aggressive behaviors are—so the behaviors are what you should focus on.

You might feel powerless but remain neutral. Save your emotional outbursts for your coach, therapist, or family, and lower your expectations for an emotionally satisfying conversation. It's probably okay to say that these experiences have been upsetting and painful, but we want the person to take action against the employee displaying bullying behaviors. In other words, we need to speak their language—the language of business.

#7: Self-reflect

There is a possibility your manager will not believe you when you tell him or her you are being bullied, so we think it's important to self-reflect and get clarity on a few things before you decide to set up that meeting. We strongly encourage you to do a little soul searching and ask yourself the questions we've outlined here.

- Are you willing to go forth without the law to back-up your claims of abuse at work?
- If your organization does not have an anti-bullying workplace policy in place, are you willing to move forward anyway?
- Are you willing to risk the frustration and stress that will develop if your complaint is ignored? Are you willing to

take on more aggression from your bullying co-worker if things don't go as expected?

- Do you have the emotional strength to stick with your complaint until it is over?
- Do you have the physical stamina to proceed?
- Are you willing to proceed in spite of the barriers you may face if your manager is not empathetic?
- What is your action plan if your complaint is unsuccessful? Where will you go from there?

We ask these questions because we want you to understand the nature of the beast. One of the biggest hurdles you will face when reporting to management or human resources is that they may not have any idea what you mean when you say you are being bullied. This concept of workplace bullying is very new to the business world, and because there are no laws against it, there hasn't been any real reason for managers and human resources to take notice or create policies to manage this kind of behavior.

If you were to report sexual harassment, on the other hand, your human resources managers can turn to a corporate policy that tells them exactly what to do, and they are also required to do it by law. That's not to make reporting sexual harassment sound like a walk in the park, because it's not. Even with laws and corporate policies on their side, many people who report sexual harassment find themselves in the same tough spot we are discussing here. Reporting bullying, then, is just that much harder in the absence of law, and we want to make sure you are educated and mentally prepared before filing a grievance. Understanding your own mental strength by answering the questions we provided will help.

Seven solutions to offer your managers

We have provided a few solutions you should consider discussing with your manager. Offering solutions when filing a complaint can help you appear to be an innovative and problem-solving type of employee. As we mentioned previously, every manager prefers to hear a solution, not just the problem.

#1: Build a more collaborative and positive workplace

Before talking to your manager about a specific individual, you might try a more global approach. Fact is, collaborative and positive workplaces perform better. The benefits of a collaborative and positive workplace include:

- Motivated, inspired, and engaged employees
- Valued internal relationships and investment in employee success
- Increased retention and reduced turnover
- Reduced absenteeism and medical leaves
- Minimized workplace politics
- Improved communication among staff and managers
- Good reputations in the community and their industries
- Better quality work produced at a quicker rate
- Healthy employees
- Employees who look forward to coming to work
- Attraction of better talent
- Happier customers
- Reduced workers' compensation claims and minimized possibility of litigation
- A supportive environment that facilitates learning
- Increased productivity

For example, in the book, *Positive Leadership: Strategies for Extraordinary Performance*, the author, Kim Cameron, talks about something called positive deviance, or extraordinary performance. Organizations that demonstrate positive deviance have employees with courage, resilience, forgiveness, compassion, optimism, trust, and integrity. These organizations have the ability to overcome challenges in ways that organizations without positivity in their culture cannot—a competitive advantage any leader worth a grain of salt is looking for.

Cameron's book offers four areas of focus for any manager who wants to build a positive and extraordinary organization, team, or department: climate, relationships, communication, and meaning.

Research has shown that positive climates allow people to have positive emotions, and positive emotions allow us to take in more information, learn, build personal resources, downplay negative emotions—such as sadness and anxiety—and enhance decision-making, productivity, and pro-social behaviors. Positive relationships and communication encourage people at work to talk to each other, share ideas, experience higher levels of energy, build trust, become more creative, foster the ability to adapt easily to changes and other challenges, and increase commitment to the organization. Finally, meaning refers to the idea that employees will work harder if they find their work to be meaningful. That doesn't mean we all have to quit our jobs and start volunteering for a non-profit; however, it does mean that if we believe in each other and in the work we are doing, then we will work harder, produce more, and reach levels of *positive deviance.*

So talk to your managers about making the workplace one where employees can thrive.

> ## Creating meaning in work
>
> A branch at a computer sales company was barely meeting its quota each month, and the VP of Sales was starting to come down on the team. Dale, the sales manager, had tried everything he could think of to bring the numbers up, but the VP advised that someone was going to be fired if things didn't shape up immediately.
>
> One day a team member, Chris, called into work to let Dale know that his wife had complications with her pregnancy, and the outlook was not certain for her or the child. Chris asked for thirty days off to be with his family, and despite Dale's plea to let him have it, the VP of Sales denied the request and gave Chris one week. After all, Chris was needed if the department was going to make their numbers.
>
> Dale decided to allow Chris thirty days off anyway, and the rest of the team covered for him. The team immediately grew to the number one place in the U.S., even before Chris returned to work. And when he did, he immediately climbed to the number one sales position, and even later won an award for bringing in the most dollars for the company that year.
>
> The VP was shocked at how well this team had performed, and figured it must have been his threat to fire someone that did the trick.
>
> Little did he know, it was the fact that the team had found meaning in their work. They worked hard to cover for Chris, because he needed the time off. And Chris worked hard to thank his team, because they had done something wonderful for him.

#2: Implement an anti-bullying, or healthy workplace, corporate policy

Of course, policies cannot wipe away bullying all on their own, but if a policy is in place it gives you a leg to stand on when you are ready to file a grievance. Suggest this first, before you file any grievances, as it might solve the problem. If the policy is implemented and doesn't stop aggressive behaviors, you can file a grievance with a policy under your belt to help you.

It may be that your managers aren't interested in implementing an actual corporate policy. Depending on your organization, that could be major process they just don't want to get involved with. But, your manager is certainly free to implement rules within your own department or work group. If a corporate policy is out of the question, try asking that a rule of civility be implemented in your department specifically.

We've included a template policy for you to show to your managers in Appendix B, if you feel it would be appropriate to do so.

#3: Seek transfer to a new department or work group

One solution might be that you simply request a move to another department or worksite. This solution will work best if you let your manager know that you have tried to work with this person, but the behavior has not changed. Of course, this is an option you have to really think through. Are you willing to change workgroups or work sites? Will you be angry that you made the switch once you do? This is an option to share with HR, but only if you're ready to follow through.

#4: Implement a 360-degree employee review process

If you find that management doesn't believe you when you talk about aggressive behaviors, ask them about doing a 360-degree review process for your department. Where most companies provide performance evaluations from the top down, a 360-degree review allows everyone to review each other. Each participant would receive an anonymous review from peers, subordinates, and superiors—and this of course would give others the chance to talk anonymously about how they feel about the person you claim is too aggressive. The outcome of the 360-degree process is that top managers will have a stronger understanding of the relationships in your department and how to make them even more effective.

#5: Get coaching or training programs

One possible solution to discuss with managers is communication and management training or coaching. Although the problems may go deeper than just your bullying coworker's communication problems, suggesting training or coaching is a solution in which most managers have experience and can easily understand.

When an employee goes through a coaching program, generally the program is tied to that employee's performance evaluation. If an aggressive employee is assigned a coaching program, then, they should be provided with goals and challenged to make a change. If the bullying goes beyond a communication skills problem, the coaching will provide the opportunity to unleash that information. You may even consider finding a coach first before talking to HR, and ask the coach to help you make the business case for a coaching program.

You may also find that offering up the idea of communication skills training for your whole department is a good place to start. We are not suggesting that a bully can attend one training event and be cured of aggressive ways forever, but a training program is a step in the right direction, and proposing it shows your manager you've been thinking about ways to assist in ending the problem.

#6: Create a respectful workplace team

Another possibility is a respectful workplace team. In fact, many organizations already have diversity and inclusion teams (D & I teams). If your organization has one, you may find that talking with them about adding bullying to their already existing programs is a good way to go. If not, talk with management about the possibility of starting a team focused on respect and civility. Just like D & I teams, your team could be responsible for holding training programs, putting together community volunteer events, and even being the go-to team for other people who are bullied. If your team lets the company know that any disrespectful behavior can be reported to them, and in turn the team will help get that information properly reported to HR, more people may step forward with their bullying complaints.

#7: Implement an anonymous reporting tool

Even if no one speaks up to you or to management, because bullying is normally a group phenomenon (as opposed to a secluded one-on-one issue) the chances that others feel bullied if you feel bullied are extremely high. If management doesn't believe there is an issue with workplace bullying, point out the benefits of a cost-effective anonymous reporting tool. A reporting tool simply requires that a link be placed on the organization's intranet. Anyone witnessing or experiencing harassment, sexual harassment, discrimination, threats of violence, violence, or bullying can then make an anonymous report about it. The report is emailed to a team of designated managers (e.g., human resources, D&I captain, high-level managers) who can then take action. This type of software is fairly inexpensive.

§

Once your conversation with HR is over, and you've laid out all of the issues, the cost of the bullying behavior, and your solutions—and have received a response from HR—you will want to return to your workspace and write down some notes regarding the following questions:

Reflection: *How did the conversation go? What did you do well? What could you have done differently, or better?*

Next Steps: *What is your action plan? What next steps will you take now that the conversation is over? If your requests for change were not met, what are your next steps? If your requests for change were met, what role will you play in them?*

On a final note, one thing you should *not* do during your conversation with HR is present an ultimatum. While it is extremely important that you know your limits and have a well-thought out bottom line for yourself, you should not share that bottom line during your complaint. Do not say that if they don't do something you will leave the organization, or will post your stories on your social media page or contact the media. Backing HR into a corner does not appear professional, and usually when people feel backed into a corner they eliminate the individual that put them there—you. If you want them to empathize with you, you have to empathize with them. We cannot stress the importance of thinking about the situation through their eyes, and making your complaint with that in mind.

CHAPTER 7: THE COST OF WORKPLACE BULLYING

Eighteen ways bullies wreak havoc on targets and organizations

Tolerating workplace bullying can result in a range of disastrous outcomes for all parties involved: the targets, the bystanders, and the organization. Bullying behaviors not only damage the morale and sanity of individual co-workers but they can also often result in great monetary losses for the organization. The information in this chapter is your key to success when talking about bullying to your managers and human resources representatives. They will respond more positively to your complaint if you can help them understand how bad bullying is for the bottom line.

It is unfortunate, but in many cases targets find their pain is not enough of a reason to address bullying in the eyes of management—but they'll listen when you can show how the bottom line suffers. What those managers are forgetting is that employees are an organization's most valuable resource, and bullying is a devastating force that severely hurts that very resource.

Several attempts have been made at estimating the actual costs of disrespectful workplace behaviors and workplace bullying. This is a difficult task because there are so many dynamics involved, and each case is so vastly different and dependent upon such factors as the size of the organization, how the issue is handled, and organizational culture. Nonetheless, here are some of the general estimates made by workplace bullying experts:

- Pioneering researcher Heinz Leymann estimated in his article, published in *Violence and Victims* in 1990, that a bully can cost a single business up to $100,000 per year per target in sick leave, reduction in work product, and time spent by management to intervene.

- Michael H. Harrison of Harrison Psychological Associates cited a study in the Orlando Business Journal that surveyed 9,000 federal employees. Of those surveyed, 57% reported they had been bullied over a two-year period, and the study estimated that these bullies had collectively cost their organizations more than $180 million (Farrell, 2002).

- The Corporate Levers Survey, a survey conducted by the Level Playing Field Institute (2007), a non-profit organization focused on innovative approaches to fairness in the workplace, estimated that the cost of unfairness to American businesses—including bullying (i.e., public humiliation)—is more than $64 billion annually.

- The American Psychological Association estimated that bullying and other types of abusive behaviors cost businesses $300 billion annually in lost productivity, absenteeism and turnover, as well as in increased medical costs (Clay, 2010).

While these numbers seem impressive, your human resources manager might not find them helpful because they are generic and estimated. We wrote this chapter to help you understand how much the bully in *your* workplace is costing *your* organization. And as

The damage bullying causes
The cost of bullying behaviors can be divided into three categories:
1. Tangible costs
2. Psychological costs
3. Lost time

we mentioned several times throughout this book, having a solid understanding of the costs of bullying to your organization will allow you to make a solid case for dealing effectively with it when talking to management.

The cost of bullying behaviors can be divided into three categories: tangible costs, psychological costs, and lost time.

Tangible Costs

Workplace bullying can result in actual monetary losses.

#1: Pertinent information withheld from—or wrong information given to—targets, that prevents them from doing their job effectively and efficiently

Bullying can include under-the-radar tactics that involve manipulation of work and intentional miscommunication. These behaviors might include the following: withholding information, leaving people out of an email sent out to other staff, not inviting others to a staff meeting so they can't participate or to keep them in the dark about certain projects, not telling some piece of information needed to get work done correctly, or purposely giving incorrect information to ensure a person does something the wrong way. All of these tactics result in work not getting done properly—or not at all—because information is not being dispersed or misinformation is being given on purpose. Anytime this happens the organization is losing money because it is affecting the performance of everyone.

In addition, if a person works with a bullying manager, it's not likely they will approach that manager with questions that need answers in order for the job to be done right. That person will ultimately make mistakes simply because he or she is scared to ask for help—rightfully so if that person is abused every time his manager is around.

Essentially, organizations committed to developing the effective communication skills of their employees are better equipped to get things done and meet organizational goals.

#2: Lost customers who were victimized by the bully

Customers are the reason businesses thrive; therefore, it is really sad AND costly when they lose customers due to an employee who uses bullying tactics in their interactions with customers. Yet the National Institute for Occupational Safety and Healthy (NIOSH) found that 11% of bullying incidents were committed against customers. Why lose a customer to an aggressive employee? That's just silly.

Regular customer service training and customer feedback can eliminate, or at least dramatically reduce, incidents of bullying.

The case of the abused business partners

At a nonprofit organization, many customers are referred by outside business partners.

Despite the fact that the business depends on these customer referrals to survive, Jerry, the manager responsible for these relationships, found a way to have power – he bullied the referrals by making them miserable and unnecessarily micromanaging the referral process. He even turned away customers just so he could show the business partners he was in control.

Unfortunately many of these partners fell into the bully's hands. They figured they didn't need this treatment, and simply found a different company to whom they could refer their customers.

#3: Lost customers who heard about the bully from unhappy former customers

Good news travels fast, but bad news travels faster. When a customer has a great experience at your company, they will share that experience with a few people. However, customers who had a bad experience often share their story with many more people. And with the availability of blogs and social networks, bad news travels like lightening. How many times have you posted stories about your bad experiences on your social networking sites?!

#4: Anger management, communication, leadership, and other types of training

Apple pickers know that they should never put a damaged apple into the crate together with the healthy apples because it will spoil the whole crate. The same is true when it comes to people: a "bad apple" can spoil the whole team's morale. To remedy this, management might opt to address the issue by providing a variety of training events. Training is helpful, but it is expensive and doesn't solve the problem unless it is embedded in a full performance program. Most trainers will charge between $1,000 and $3,000 just for a half-day training program, which can prove to be a waste of time and money on something that could have been prevented by dealing directly with the "bad apple" immediately when the bullying behavior started.

#5: Increased presenteeism, absenteeism, and turnover; unemployment insurance

Targets often dread going to work. They call in sick, or come up with all kinds of reasons not to go. In fact, targets of bullying take an average of a full week more sick leave than employees who are not targets of bullying (Hoel & Cooper, 2000). Many will just keep taking days off until they lose their jobs.

When targets do come to work, they are often distracted by their situation and fear of the bully and don't get much done. This is called "presenteeism"—the employee is at work physically but is mentally unengaged. An employee going through a divorce, for example, would also contribute to presenteeism, meaning that while he is at work he is likely spending most of the day not thinking about how to complete tasks but thinking about his divorce. He might even be doing tasks related to the divorce, such as preparing a financial document for his attorney. In the same way, a target of bullying, and all of the people who witness the bullying on a regular basis, are likely spending time at work talking to each other about the bullying, and while at their desks are spending a lot of time thinking about the bullying, and perhaps documenting the bullying instances or looking for new jobs, instead of working.

The effects of bullying on presenteeism were made clear in a study by researchers Pearson, Anderssen, and Portah (as cited in Glendinning, 2001):

> "Individuals' experiences of incivility can have substantial bottom-line impact for organizations. When employees are on the receiving end of an uncivil encounter, they adjust their work accordingly. More than one-half of the targets in our sample reported that they lost work time because they were worrying about the uncivil incident that had occurred... More than one-forth acknowledged that they wasted work time trying to avoid the instigator... More than one-third of

those responding reported that they intentionally reduced their commitments to the organization as a result of being the target of uncivil behavior."

Ultimately, if the bullying isn't addressed many targets opt to quit their job or are let go, leaving the organization vulnerable to the costs associated with high turnover and unemployment insurance.

Turnover refers to the cycle each employee goes through, from being hired and trained, working for some period of time, leaving, and being replaced. Turnover is costly for an organization because of the time and resources spent on training an employee and then on replacing them. When a person leaves an organization, everyone must step in and work over-time to make up for that person's absence. Managers or human resources must spend time and money recruiting, interviewing, and hiring a new employee. Once that individual is hired, managers, human resources, and long-time employees must all get involved in training the new employee. Until that employee is fully trained, the employee is not working at full-speed or at top quality, and this costs the organization money.

In fact, many estimate the time it takes for a new employee to become fully integrated into an organization can be as long as nine months or more, depending on the complexity of the position. That's nine months a person is not working at full capacity. With all of these factors combined, it is estimated that turnover can cost an organization between 25% and 65% of the position's annual salary. For a position being paid $75,000 in annual salary, that's between $18,750 and $48,750! That's a lot of wasted time, effort, and money, especially if this process has to be repeated over and over. All this can be prevented—and it should be basic business common sense—by addressing the bully's behavior.

Charlotte Rayner, one of the leading workplace bullying researchers who is located in the United Kingdom, found that 27% of targets who are bullied do leave their jobs (1997). Lyn Quine, who has conducted several studies on workplace bullying in the health care industry, found in his survey of 1,100 employees that staff who were bullied reported significantly lower levels of job satisfaction, and higher levels of stress, depression, anxiety, and intention to leave their jobs (1999). Researchers Dieter Zapf and Claudia Gross reported in their article (2001) that 22% of targets told others in the same situation to leave the organization, rather than stay and try to defend themselves.

On the other hand, the American Psychological Association found that the winners of their prestigious Psychologically Healthy Workplace Awards reported an average turnover rate of only 9% in 2009, versus the national average of 41%, according to the Department of Labor's Bureau of Labor Statistics. (Winners of this award are acknowledged for their emphasis on employee involvement, work-life balance, employee growth and development, health and safety, and employee recognition.) In addition, only 12% of the employees in the winning organizations said they would seek employment elsewhere within the next year, while the national average is 31% (Clay, 2010).

Turnover is bound to happen, particularly these days when the average time spent in a job is three to five years. Turnover should ideally be under 15%, and when it gets to be 30%, 40%, 50% it should be a wake-up call for managers that there is a problem.

#6: Increased health insurance costs and workers' compensation

Many targets seek information about their mental and physical state in response to feeling so stressed out about work, and obtain paperwork from a doctor that allows them to file for workers' compensation and take leave. Of course, the more the health of employees decline, the more they file for workers' compensation, and the more expensive workers' compensation insurance becomes for the organization.

#7: Bad reputation in the industry and business community

We live in an age when competitors pop up left and right, like mushrooms after rain. Therefore, a company's reputation is one of its most valuable attraction factors. However, when this reputation is tarnished by news of bullying—with internal and external customers—today, more than ever, people can opt to go to the competitor down the street. Getting the reputation of an organization that allows bullying WILL result in substantial loss of repeat customers and vast loss or profits.

Check out www.eBossWatch.com, a high traffic site with an average of 150,000 visitors per month. (Wow! People are really paying attention) This website is a place for all to go and post their experiences with their horrible bosses, not to mention they regularly post news articles they find online about bad places to work. eBossWatch has made it their mission to hold companies and their abusive employees publicly accountable.

In addition, with the popularity of social media, rumors of bullying spread lightning fast and can prevent an organization from recruiting top-notch employees. "Employees should recognize that when a bullied employee leaves their organization, they take with them the bitter memories to their next employer. This will in all certainty gain the prior employer a bad reputation as a hostile workplace and will therefore make recruitment significantly more difficult and it will lead to a skill shortage within the workplace" (Ellis, as cited in Glendinning, 2001).

#8: Decreased shareholder returns

The term "total shareholder returns" refers to the change in value of a company over time, or the total return of stocks to an investor. Shareholder returns are related to a company's performance—when employees are performing at their best, often the total shareholder returns, or the amount of money the organization is worth, increases. For example, if all of the customer service representatives are happy and healthy, that happiness will bleed into how they treat customers. They will greet customers with a smile and do their best to help customers get what they need. Those customers, who were treated well, will tell their friends and this in turn results in new customers, and increased shareholder returns.

On the other hand, when customer service representatives are unhappy or mistreated by their managers, that too will bleed into how they treat customers. Customers will be greeted with a grumpy and uninterested tone of voice, and probably will not get all of the help they need from an unhappy employee. As a result, those customers will tell their friends, and may even find a new company with friendlier customer service, and this in turn results in a reduced number of customers and decreased shareholder returns.

In a study looking at effective communication in organizations, conducted by global consulting firm Watson Wyatt (Yates, 2006), total return to shareholders was 57% higher in organizations with effective communication than in those without, and market premium (extent to which market value exceeds costs of assets, which reflects ability to generate profits) was almost 20% higher. In this study, effective communication referred to several factors, including strong leadership during change, providing employees with communication about rewards, providing employees with financial information, and helping employees understand the business.

#9: Legal costs for counsel, litigation, and settlement fees

We are a litigious society, with companies paying out billions of dollars every year to resolve the many law suits that people file against them for accidents, wrongful termination, or discrimination. With workplace bullying getting more attention in the media and in state and city governments, organizations today face a fairly new type of litigation—having to pay out millions of dollars to bullied targets for such things as wrongful termination or intentional infliction of emotional distress. (Can you believe some bullies are fired for their behavior and also sue for wrongful termination?)

The cost of litigation is a major one. While there is no way to give an exact number, because all cases are one of a kind, the UCLA-RAND Center for Law and Public Policy released a study that described the "average" defense costs and jury awards in California employment law discrimination cases (Blasi & Doherty). So you have an understanding of what legal action might cost an employer, we thought it important to provide the information to you:

- The median settlement is $7,500
- The median legal costs to an employer through trial are $150,000. Even if the case goes to summary judgment—meaning a judge dismisses the charges before going to trial—the employer's legal costs are about $75,000
- The median award for plaintiffs is in the low six figures

Psychological Costs

From the standpoint of an individual feeling abused at work, the greatest damage a bully inflicts on his or her targets is the living in constant fear. This constant horror often results in lack of focus, increased stress levels, and inability to complete tasks appropriately and in a timely manner. While we know the psychological effects of bullying go much deeper, for a manager or human resources representative it's the toll on organizational performance that matters. Some of the effects bullying can have on targets and witnesses of the behavior, which you may be able to discuss with managers, are as follows:

#10: Loss of motivation and energy

When coming to work means facing yet another day of torment, it often results in total loss of motivation and development of chronic fatigue. Nobody wants to work when they fear their bullying boss or coworker, or are walking on eggshells just waiting for the next attack. Motivation to get work done is out the window. Employees who work with a bully are motivated instead to stay under the radar and avoid interaction with the bully as much as possible.

#11: Stress induced psychological and physical illness

If the bullying is allowed to go on for an extended period, the target of bullying can develop a variety of psychological and physical symptoms, ranging from stomach ulcers to depression and even PTSD (Posttraumatic Stress Disorder), as discussed in earlier chapters. When untreated, the lives of these individuals can be wrecked for years or even for a lifetime. Unfortunately, some resort to the ultimate "solution" of suicide.

To help you deliver a clear picture to your managers of what bullying does to a target's psychological well-being, we thought we would provide a few research articles here. Please note that the number of scientific research articles that have connected bullying to psychological and physical detriment are abundant—there are literally hundreds, if not thousands, of articles published in hundreds of peer-reviewed scientific journals. Not to mention the thousands of conversations workplace bullying researchers, consultants and therapists, including us, have had with targets that further confirm that what the research

Seek help

If you are feeling so stressed out at work that you cannot get anything done, are showing up late or not at all, and feel depressed and anxious about interactions at work, then you should seek assistance from your doctor—and if needed, take a medical leave to clear your head and make decisions about your work situation.

has to say is accurate. The damage bullying causes is simply unquestionable.

In a study commissioned by the French government and conducted by four French Occupational Pathology Centers, counselors conducted an interview with targets of bullying to learn about their state of mind, and then a second interview 12 months later. The Clermont-Ferrand Occupational Pathology Center published its research in a journal called *Occupational Medicine* (Brousse, G., Fontana, L., Ouchchane, et al, 2008), and found that at the first interview 52% of targets showed symptoms of depression and 83% showed symptoms of anxiety.

Clinical signs observed were dysphoria, insomnia, reduced libido, and feeling alienated. In addition, one in four interviewees reported thoughts of suicide, while one in two reported a deep fear of returning to work. Twelve months later, at the second interview, these targets reported somatic symptoms and disorders, including weight gain, digestive disorders, heart palpitations, migraines, and muscular pain. These targets also reported feelings of shame, guilt, and loss in self-confidence.

Researchers Zapf, Knorz, and Kulla found in their research, published in the *European Journal of Work and Organisational Psychology* (1996), that 54% of their research participants had to receive medical treatment for the stress they were feeling as a result of being bullied. In addition, 55% of them had taken three or more periods of sick leave during the previous 12 months, and 24% of them said they had used long-term sick leave to get away from the bully and try to cope with their experiences.

World-renowned bullying researcher Vartia found in her study, published in the *Scandinavian Journal of Work and Environmental Health* (2001), that 40% of targets of bullying experienced much more stress in comparison to bystanders, but that 25% of the bystanders did feel stress as a result of the bullying. She also found that 30% of the bullied employees in her research were using sleep-inducing drugs and sedatives, and that 18% of bystanders were doing the same.

We know you don't need research to understand how you feel and what damage bullying has caused you—but you may find that reading about the science on the topic will give you a better understanding of WHY you experience psychological changes and physical ailments. And this information will help you in talking with others about your pain and convincing them that it is real.

#12: Decreased work quality and quantity; decreased employee performance

As a result of all of the psychological problems one who is bullied suffers, work quality suffers, mistakes sneak in, time is spent worrying about the next attack, and loyalty to the company and managers drops to zero.

Plain and simple—people can't get quality work done when they work in an environment of fear and are feeling panicked, stressed, irritable, and depressed.

#13: Lost innovation and ability to learn

In an article published in the *Harvard Business Review* (2008), authors Garvin, Edmondson, and Gino discuss the pinnacle of innovation in an organization—a supportive learning environment. As they point out, in order for employees to learn new things, and thus stretch beyond themselves and be innovative, a culture of psychological safety, appreciation of differences, openness to new ideas, and time for reflection must exist. In other words, if people don't feel safe to speak up, and instead fear getting belittled or made fun of, then they won't express their ideas or points of view. If employees won't take risks because they are concerned about the lack of openness to them, then they won't bother to be innovative.

Innovation and learning is important to an organization because without them, an organization can't grow or meet the ever-changing demands of customers.

#14: Counterproductive workplace behavior

Counterproductive workplace behaviors (CWB) violate an organization's norms and are contrary to what the organization and its members would normally consider ethical and acceptable. Examples of CWB include stealing office supplies, showing up late, and violating corporate policies. These behaviors are considered CWB when they are on purpose and geared toward getting back at the organization for some perceived injustice such as pay, denial of a vacation day, or being overlooked for a promotion. CWB manifests in order to relieve the imbalance the perpetrator feels between what they believe they deserve and what they believe they are actually receiving. CWB is often categorized into two sectors: CWB aimed at the organization (e.g., stealing or destruction of company equipment), and CWB aimed at individuals (e.g., abuse or other anti-social behavior).

For example, researchers Jensen, Opland, and Ryan (2009) point out in their research that when employees perceive that an organization has violated some contract or promise made, they will indeed engage in CWB in retaliation in the form of abusing others. These researchers also looked at the relationship between violation of economic promises (i.e., pay raise) and CWB, and found that employees will make threats to those they thought responsible for the breach of promise.

We bring up CWB for two reasons. The first being that some targets may engage in CWB such as stealing office supplies or spending hours surfing social media sites during work hours in order to help overcome feelings of unfairness and injustice as a result of being bullied. And who can blame them! It's only natural that some people rebel against their oppressor. If you've talked to your manager about bullying and they aren't helping, then looking for a new job while you're clocked in seems like a fair deal to us. Unfortunately, your manager won't see it that way. So of course we don't recommend that you tell your manager that one of the costs of bullying is that you aren't doing your work. However, your bully is also engaging in CWB, so the second reason we mention CWB is that we certainly suggest you bring it up to management.

Unfortunately, we cannot tell you that one employee engaging in CWB will cost your organization some specific number of dollars. To our knowledge, there isn't any research that would allow us to give you that information. But, we did want to familiarize you with the term because it relates to bullying, and we think we can all agree that CWB does indeed cost an organization's bottom line, even if we can't quantify it.

Lost Time

Time is a precious commodity. There are only 24 hours, or 1,440 minutes, in a day. Each one of these minutes wasted as a result of bullying are minutes that we never get back. Any manager will agree that lost time is lost productivity. Time is money, right? So here are some of the time-wasters bullies cause:

#15: Time spent by co-workers and managers calming and counseling targets, or gossiping about the behavior

A side effect of allowing bullying to go on in the workplace is that people start wasting productive time on talking about the bully or the target, the "stunts" the bully pulls regularly, and other distracting conversations—ultimately resulting in lost productivity and lower morale.

Others might spend valuable time listening to targets recount their experiences, whether behind closed doors just to vent or when a formal grievance is filed. These employees become the target's "go-to person" for regular ad hoc counseling.

The Canada Safety Council, for example, reported that people who are bullied at work spend up to 52% of their day dealing with the repercussions of bullying, rather than working (2000). In another example, researchers Hoel and Cooper (2000) found that 63% of targets of bullying spent time discussing the bullying at work with colleagues.

#16: Time spent by management appeasing, counseling, or disciplining bullies

Some organizations provide great support to targets but fail to address the bullying behaviors. That is to say they treat the symptoms, but fail to address the disease. Trying to help people adjust their behaviors is a crucial part of creating a bully-free workplace. While it does take time away from productive output, it is vital to go to the source of all trouble and do whatever it takes to make the bullying stop. If this step is done correctly, the whole organization wins; there'll be less stress, less time spent on gossiping and complaining, fewer people spending time looking for new jobs, fewer errors on the job, and a ton of other benefits.

#17: Time spent reorganizing departments and teams

If management decides that one way to remedy the turmoil created by bullying behavior is to separate the targets from the perpetrators, teams often find themselves reorganized. This creates the need to re-train people and allow them to get used to the change, and we can only hope that the new setup will work out as expected. Fact is, however, that reorganizing teams is often like treating the symptom, while the cancer—the person displaying the bullying behavior—is still there and will most likely sicken the new work team just as he did before.

#18: Time spent by targets looking for different work

If management doesn't do anything to stop the bullying—or if the bullies are in top management positions—it is only a matter of time before the target and other employees who are frustrated with what they experience or witness start looking for a new job...often during work hours, further deflecting precious time that could have been spent on productive tasks.

Conclusion

"Imagine all the people
Living life in peace"

~ John Lennon ~

Imagine living in a world where we all treated each other with respect. A world without bullies, small-minded people, or any kind of jerks. No yelling, no humiliation, no gossip. Imagine a world where going to work is about accomplishing tasks and about self-fulfillment…and…well, a little money making.

It's nice to imagine such a world, but the harsh reality is that difficult people aren't going anywhere anytime soon; and while we can't change the people around us, we can always change our reaction to them. When we change our reaction to them, we change our situation to a positive one.

After all, contrary to what the media portrays, people who bully are not evil psychopaths. With a little help—and by making them aware that their behaviors are unacceptable—anyone can choose to improve and become better co-workers or managers.

When dealing with bullying, we all have the power to react, overreact, or be passive in response to behaviors that we perceive as difficult. Many respond to these atrocious behaviors with passivity: suffering in silence and enabling the bully to continue his or her quest to make everyone's life miserable. Others overreact to the bully's behaviors and take revenge—often, unfortunately, taking their revenge by bullying others. Violence begets violence. Overreacting to the bullying behavior is more damaging in the long run for everyone involved.

Just as a pebble rolling down from the top of a mountain can start a whole avalanche, the same is true when it comes to bullying. If someone doesn't stop this "pebble"—that is, the initial bullying behaviors—the negative effects can take on the magnitude of an avalanche, with dire effects on you, your co-workers, and your entire organization.

Choose to be part of the solution. Take what you learned in the pages of this book and reclaim your peace of mind. There is no reason for you to suffer as a result of someone else's ignorance or ill ways, but there are countless reasons why you should take action to stop the bully from tormenting you or your co-workers. You have the tools; the rest is up to you.

You can do it—we believe in you. Believe in yourself.

Appendix A: Worksheet -
Preparing to Talk with Management

Instructions: Fill out this worksheet to get prepared to talk to your manager about the bullying behaviors. Use Chapter 6 as a guide. Note that this worksheet itself should not be provided to managers, this worksheet is meant to help you prepare.

Fill out this part before your conversation with HR or management

Document what happened: Use this chart as a guide as you write in your journal about the bullying behaviors you've witnessed. Remember to focus on the behaviors, not on your emotions.

Date of bullying incident	Description of event. Be as detailed as possible. (e.g., What was said? What was the body language like? Where did it occur?)	Names of witnesses	Supporting documents (e.g., emails, performance evaluations, etc.)

Additional documents you will bring with you to the meeting (e.g., doctor's notes, articles about bullying, personnel records, etc.):

1._____
2._____
3._____
4._____
5._____
6._____

Proof of your good performance: What proof can you provide that you are a good performer?

_____
_____
_____

Names of people who have agreed to vouch for your performance:

1._____
2._____
3._____
4._____

Documents you can provide to prove your good performance:

1._____
2._____
3._____
4._____

Address previous performance evaluations: If you have received poor employee evaluations, what have you done to attempt to gain clarity on your performance? What dates did you reach out to your manager for clarification on your performance?

What was the response? (If you sent emails, be sure to print them out for your files.)

Dates	Response (Ignored? Or was a meeting set?)

If you do get a meeting with your manager, be sure to answer the following questions during the meeting:

- What exact behaviors are needed to improve?

  _____

  _____

  _____

- What specific goals can you set to improve your performance?

  _____

  _____

  _____

- When do the goals you set need to be accomplished?

  _____

  _____

  _____

- What measure of success can you present to prove the goal was reached?

  _____

  _____

  _____

- What resources will be provided to ensure you meet your goals?

  _____

  _____

  _____

- What are the consequences if you do not meet them?

  _____

  _____

  _____

Costs to the organization: What real, tangible costs of bullying can you present to the manager? Use Chapter 7 as a guide.

Description	Estimated cost
Ex: Customer who cancelled services because they were bullied	*$10,000*
Total estimated cost	

Actions: What actions have you taken to attempt to rectify the behavior on your own?

Date of actions taken by you	Description of your actions (be as detailed as possible)	Witnesses	Supporting Documents (e.g., emails, documented discussions with immediate manager, etc.)

Understand your goals: Why are you having this conversation? What do you want to accomplish? Do you want the organization to take action against the aggressor? Transfer you to a new department? By what date do you need to see action?

_____

_____

_____

_____

_____

Expected Outcomes: How will you know you've accomplished what you needed to accomplish? How will you know the goals you set for the conversation were reached? What will you do if they are not reached? Which goals are you willing to give up?

_____

_____

_____

_____

Develop communication strategies: List some thoughts on ways you want to "be" during the interaction in order for you to achieve your goal. How will you present yourself during the conversation? What confident body language will you focus on? What words will you use or avoid?

_____

_____

_____

_____

_____

_____

Self-Reflection: Are you willing to make a complaint without laws or a corporate policy on your side? Are you willing to risk the frustration if your complaint is ignored? Are you willing to take on more aggression from your bullying co-worker if things don't go as expected? Do you have the emotional strength to stick with your complaint until it is over? Are you willing to proceed in spite of the barriers you may face if your manager is not empathetic? What is your action plan if your complaint is unsuccessful? Where will you go from there?

_____

_____

_____

_____

_____

_____

_____

_____

Solutions: What solutions will you offer the manager? How can the organization assist you in addressing your situation successfully?

Description of solution	Why is this a good solution? How can this help?	What part, if any, will you play in implementing the solution?

Additional Notes:

Fill out this part after your conversation with HR or management

Once the conversation is over, we recommend that you complete the following reflections as soon as possible. Doing so will help you understand what happened during the conversation, if you found it helpful or not, and what your next steps might be.

Reflection: How did the conversation go? What did you do well? What could you have done differently, or better? What changes did management commit to or promise?

_____

_____

_____

_____

_____

_____

Next Steps: What next steps will you take now that the conversation is over? If your requests for change were not met, what are your next steps? If your requests for change were met, what role will you play in them?

_____

_____

_____

_____

_____

_____

_____

_____

Appendix B: Respectful Workplace Corporate Policy Template

Provide this template policy to your managers.

Company and Management Commitment

It is the commitment of this company and its management to ensure this place of work is free from negative, aggressive, and inappropriate behaviors, and that the environment is aimed at providing high quality products and services in an atmosphere of respect, collaboration, openness, safety, and equality. All employees have the right to be treated with dignity and respect. (These terms are used interchangeably throughout this policy.)

All complaints of negative and inappropriate workplace behaviors will be taken seriously and followed through to resolution, and employees who file complaints will not be victimized for "whistle-blowing" or reporting others for their behavior.

Scope

Protection from negative, aggressive, and inappropriate behaviors extends to management, fellow employees, subordinates, clients, customers, and other business contacts and expands beyond the place of work to off-site and work-related social events. It is the responsibility of all employees and managers of this company to provide a healthy workplace environment to peers and co-workers, where all communication and interactions are marked by dignity and respect.

Acceptable and Healthy Workplace Behaviors Defined

Acceptable and healthy workplace behaviors include, but are not limited to:

- Using respectful, supportive, and encouraging language in all interactions, no matter the subject of conversation
- Questioning a peer's position on an issue politely rather than asserting your position is the right one; listening to your peer's position with an open mind
- Giving peers direct, non-personal feedback as opposed to criticism
- Expressing appreciation when a peer does something correctly and in a timely manner
- Respecting each other as adults and trusting their decision making abilities
- Approaching conflict with maturity and true desire for resolution, rather than as a fight or opportunity to belittle a co-worker
- Maintaining a positive attitude, even when you are having a bad day

Unacceptable and Inappropriate Behaviors Defined

These behaviors are defined as negative and even aggressive acts aimed at one or more individuals and causing them to feel hurt, embarrassed, incompetent, disrespected, anxious, or depressed. Examples include, but are not limited to:

- Excessive yelling, repeated emotional outbursts, berating others, using a harsh tone of voice
- Talking down to others or using degrading remarks or tone of voice
- Criticizing or talking down to others in front of a group; using a condescending tone

- Social exclusion or ostracism, ignoring others, silent treatment
- Treating some less favorably than others
- Undermining another's work by giving impossible to meet deadlines or workloads
- Excessive monitoring of work or unnecessary micromanagement
- Arbitrary or punitive punishment
- Withholding pertinent work-related information; undermining another's work by not giving them enough information to do what is required of them
- Gossiping or spreading rumors
- Manipulating a person's job content; unwarranted removal of core responsibilities
- Blaming others for things out of their control
- Making threats; using intimidating tactics
- Any malicious behavior a reasonable person would find unprofessional, disturbing, and harmful to their psychological health

These types of behaviors are well recognized as having damaging consequences for their recipients, the observers of the behavior, and the organization as a whole, and are therefore not tolerated.

Management Responsibility

Management and others in positions of authority and workplace representatives have a particular responsibility to ensure that healthy and appropriate behaviors are being exhibited at all times and that complaints to the contrary are addressed speedily. Management will:

- Provide good examples by treating all with courtesy and respect

- Promote awareness of the policy and complaint procedures
- Be vigilant for signs of inappropriate behaviors at work through observation and information seeking, and take action to resolve the behavior before it escalates
- Deal sensitively with employees involved in a complaint, whether as complainant or alleged aggressor
- Explain the procedures to be followed if a complaint of inappropriate behavior at work is made
- Ensure that an employee making a complaint is not victimized for doing so, and seek resolution of such behavior if it occurs
- Monitor and follow up the situation after a complaint is made so as to prevent recurrence of the behavior.

Employee Responsibility

Employees can contribute to achieving a work environment that does not tolerate aggressive behavior at work. Employees should report what they see in the workplace as it relates to behaviors defined as unacceptable; employees are in a far better position than management to know what is happening with peers and co-workers. Employees should also co-operate with preventative measures introduced by management, and recognize that a finding of unacceptable behaviors at work will be dealt with through appropriate disciplinary procedures. Equally, a finding of vexatious complaints will also be dealt with through appropriate disciplinary procedures.

Training Programs

As part of its commitment to encouraging positive and healthy behaviors, the company has established training programs for all employees and managers. Training is included as part of the new hire orientation, and thereafter annually as scheduled by the company. Training will identify factors that contribute to a bully-free environment, familiarize participants with responsibilities under this policy, and provide steps to overcoming a bullying incident, including filing an adequate and informed report to the appropriate party.

Process for Investigation of Complaints

The aim and objectives of a formal complaint process include a thorough investigation of allegations of negative, aggressive, and inappropriate behaviors; written documentation from all parties involved; and resolution in a timely manner. Resolution will include any number and combination of possibilities, depending upon the outcome of the complaint process (e.g., training, disciplinary actions, transfer of employees involved, etc.).

Any employee or manager seeking to file a complaint against an alleged aggressor should take special care to ensure the complaint is confined to and consists of precise details of each incident of negative, aggressive, and inappropriate behaviors, including dates, times, locations, and any witnesses. Formal complaints should be filed with a Human Resources Representative (HRR), and should be documented in writing.

The person complained against will be notified in writing by the HRR that an allegation has been made against him or her, and assured of the organization's presumption of innocence at this juncture.

The HRR receiving the complaint or another representative from Human Resources will act as an investigator, unless otherwise specified by management. The objective of the investigation is to ascertain whether or not the behaviors complained of occurred, and therefore will include interviewing the person complained of, witnesses, managers, and any other party that may be involved with or witness to the alleged behaviors. All interviews will be documented in writing in order to maintain clarity throughout the investigation. The investigation will be conducted thoroughly, objectively, with sensitivity and utmost confidentiality, and with due respect for the rights of both the complainant and the alleged aggressor. The investigation will be completed as quickly as possible.

Upon completion of the investigation, the investigator will submit a report to management or another party deemed appropriate at the outset of the complaint that will include the investigator's conclusions.

The employer will decide in light of the investigator's report and follow up comments by the parties what, if any, action will be taken. The HRR will inform the complainant and the person complained against in writing of the action plan, and each will have the opportunity to appeal the report and/or the action plan. Appeals should include a detailed outline of the reason for the appeal in writing, and should be submitted to and heard by another party that did not participate in the initial report or investigation as designated by management.

Where a complaint has been upheld, management will follow appropriate disciplinary procedures and decide what action in regards to the complaint is necessary. The employer will continue to keep the situation under review, and may provide counseling for the complainant where appropriate. Preventative measures will also be taken to ensure elimination of the hazard in the future and reduce effects of the prior exposure.

References

American Institute of Stress. (n.d.). *Effects of Stress.* Retrieved December 21, 2010 from: http://www.stress.org/topic-effects.htm

American Psychological Association. (n.d.). *The road to resilience.* Retrieved March 12, 2012, from http://www.apa.org/helpcenter/road-resilience.aspx

Ashforth, B.E. (1994). Petty tyranny in organizations. *Human Relations, 47,* 755-778.

Blanchard, K., & Johnson, S. (1982). *The One Minute Manager.* New York: Berkley Books.

Blasi, G., & Doherty, J.W. (n.d.). California employment discrimination law and its enforcement: The Fair Employment and Housing Act at 50. *UCLA-RAND Center for Law and Public Policy.* Retrieved October 21, 2010, from: http://dfeh.ca.gov/res/docs/Renaissance/FEHA%20at%2050%20-%20UCLA%20-%20RAND%20Report_FINAL.pdf

Blosser, F. (2004, Jul 28). Most workplace bullying is worker to worker, early findings from NIOSH study suggest. *National Institute for Occupational Safety and Health.* Retrieved October 10, 2010 from: http://www.cdc.gov/niosh/updates/upd-07-28-04.html

Britton, K. (2009, Apr 7). Powerful questions to ask in a job interview. *Positive Psychology News Daily.* Retrieved July 8, 2011, from: http://positivepsychologynews.com/news/kathryn-britton/200904071593

Brousse, G., Fontana, L., Ouchchane, L., Boisson, C., Gerbaud, L., Bourguet, D., et al. (2008). Psychopathological features of a patient population of targets of workplace bullying. *Occupational Medicine, 58,* 122-128.

Cameron, K. (2008). *Positive leadership: Strategies for extraordinary performance.* San Francisco: Berrett-Koehler.

Canadian Centre for Occupational Health and Safety. (n.d.). *Violence in the Workplace – Warning Signs.* Retrieved May 13, 2012, from:

http://www.ccohs.ca/oshanswers/psychosocial/violence_warning_si
gns.html

Canada Safety Council. (2000). *Bullying in the workplace.* Retrieved
October 21, 2010, from: http://canadasafetycouncil.org/workplace-
safety/bullying-workplace

Clay, R.A. (2010). Healthier workplaces and better bottom lines.
American Psychological Association. Retrieved April 30, 2011,
from: http://www.apa.org/monitor/2010/05/slc-workplaces.aspx

Denenberg, R.V., & Braverman, M. (1999). *The Violence-Prone
Workplace: A New Approach to Dealing with Hostile, Threatening,
and Uncivil Behavior.* Ithaca, NY: Cornell University Press.

Einarsen, S. (1999). The nature and causes of bullying at work.
International Journal of Manpower, 20, 16-27.

Einarsen, S., & Raknes, B.I. (1997). Harassment in the workplace and the
victimization of men. *Violence and Victims, 12*(2), 247-263.

Escartin, J., Rodriquez-Carballeira, A., Zapf, D., Porrua, C., & Martin-
Pena, J. (2009). Perceived severity of various bullying behaviors at
work and the relevance of exposure to bullying. *Work & Stress,
23*(3), 191-205.

Ethics Resource Center. (2010). *Blowing the Whistle on Workplace
Misconduct.* Retrieved January 5, 2011, from:
http://www.ethics.org/files/u5/WhistleblowerWP.pdf

Farrell, L.U. (2002, March 15). Workplace bullying's high cost: $180M
in lost time, productivity. *Orlando Business Journal.* Retrieved May
1, 2010 from:
http://orlando.bizjournals.com/orlando/stories/2002/03/18/focus1.ht
ml?page=1

Garvin, D.A., Edmondson, A.C., & Gino, F. (2008). Is yours a learning
organization? *Harvard Business Review, Mar,* 109-116.

Glendinning, P.M. (2001). Workplace bullying: Curing the cancer of the
American workplace. *Public Personnel Management, 30*(3), 269-
286.

Grasz, J. (2011). One-in-four workers have felt bullied in the workplace,
CareerBuilder study finds. *CareerBuilder.com.* Retrieved May 14,
2012, from:

http://www.careerbuilder.com/share/aboutus/pressreleasesdetail.asp
x?id=pr632&sd=4%2F20%2F2011&ed=4%2F20%2F2099

Hirschfeld, S.J. (2007). Nearly 45% of US workers say they've worked
for an abusive boss. *Employment Law Alliance.* Retrieved October
10, 2010 from
http://www.employmentlawalliance.com/en/node/1810

Hoel, H., & Cooper, C.L. (2000). Survey report: Destructive conflict and
bullying at work. Sponsored by the British Occupational Health
Research Foundation and Manchester School of Management.

Horn, S. (1996). *Tongue Fu! How to Deflect, Disarm, and Defuse Any
Verbal Conflict.* New York: St. Martin's.

Jensen, J.M., Opland, R.A., & Ryan, A.M. (2009). Psychological
contracts and counterproductive work behaviors: Employee
responses to transactional and relational breach. *Journal of Business
Psychology, 25,* 555-568.

Kawasaki, G. (2007, Apr 10). LinkedIn and the Art of Avoiding an
Asshole Boss. Retrieved May 17, 2012, from:
http://blog.guykawasaki.com/2007/04/linkedin_and_th.html#axzz1u
fmtWqUt

Labour Relations Commission. (n.d.). *Code of Practice: Procedures for
Addressing Bullying in the Workplace.* Retrieved May 14, 2012,
from:
http://www.lrc.ie/viewdoc.asp?m=7&fn=/documents/publications/c
odes/6Bullying.pdf

Level Playing Field Institute. (2007). *Corporate Leavers Survey.*
Retrieved October 10, 2010 from
http://www.lpfi.org/workplace/corporateleavers.html

Leymann, H. (1990). Mobbing and psychological terror at workplaces.
Violence and Victims, 5(2), 119-126.

Matthiesen, S.B., & Einarsen, S. (2004). Psychiatric distress and
symptoms of PTSD among victims of bullying at work. *British
Journal of Guidance & Counselling, 32,* 335-356.

Matthiesen, S.B., Einarsen, S. (2007). Perpetrators and targets of bullying
at work: Role stress and individual differences. *Violence and
Victims, 22,* 735-744, 747-753.

Mattice, C.M. (2007). Bullies in business: A self-report survey of behavior rationale. Unpublished master's thesis, San Diego State University, San Diego, CA, United States.

McEllistrem, J.E. (2004). Affective and predatory violence: A bimodal classification system of human aggression and violence. *Aggression and Violent Behavior, 10,* 1-30.

Namie, G., & Namie, R. (2009). *The Bully at Work: What You Can Do to Stop the Hurt and Reclaim Your Dignity on the Job, 2nd Ed.* Naperville, IL: Sourcebooks.

Occupational Safety & Health Administration (OSHA). (n.d.). *Workplace violence.* Retrieved May 14, 2012, from: http://www.osha.gov/SLTC/workplaceviolence/

Quine, L. (1999). Workplace bullying in NHS community trust: Staff questionnaire survey. *British Medical Journal, 318,* 228–232.

Rayner, C. (1997). The incidence of workplace bullying. *Journal of Community & Applied Social Psychology, 7,* 199-208.

Smith, P.K., Singer, M., Hoel, H., Cooper, C.L. (2003). Victimization in the school and the workplace: Are there any links? *British Journal of Psychology, 94,* 175-188.

Spitzberg, B.H. (1983). Communication competence as knowledge, skill and impression. *Communication Education, 32,* 323-329.

Sutton, R.I. (2007). *The No Asshole Rule: Building a Civilized Workplace and Surviving One That Isn't.* New York: Business Plus.

Tracy, S.J., Lutgen-Sandvik, P., & Alberts, J.K. (2006). Nightmares, demons and slaves: Exploring the painful metaphors of workplace bullying. *Management Communication Quarterly, 20,* 148-185.

University of California, San Francisco. (n.d.). *Dealing with threatening or potentially violent behavior.* Retrieved October 21, 2010, from: http://ucsfhr.ucsf.edu/index.php/pubs/hrguidearticle/appendix-d-dealing-with-threatening-or-potentially-violent-behavior/

Vartia, M. (1996). The sources of bullying – psyhcological work environment and organizational climate. *European Journal of Work and Organizational Psychology, 5,* 203-214.

Vartia, M. (2001). Consequences of workplace bullying with respect to the well-being of its targets and the observers of bullying. *Scandinavian Journal of Work and Environmental Health, 27*(1), 63-69.

Vega, G., & Comer, D.R. (2005). Sticks and stones may break your bones, but words can break your spirit: Bullying in the workplace. *Journal of Business Ethics, 58,* 101-109.

The Workplace Bullying Institute. (n.d.). *Results of the 2010 and 2007 WBI U.S. Bullying Survey.* Retrieved May 14, 2012, from: http://www.workplacebullying.org/wbiresearch/2010-wbi-national-survey/

Yates, K. (2006). Internal communication effectiveness enhances bottom-line results. *Journal of Organizational Excellence,* 71-79.

Zapf, D., & Gross, C. (2001). Conflict escalation and coping with workplace bullying: A replication and extension. *European Journal of Work and Organizational Psychology, 10*(4), 497-522.

Zapf, D., Knorz, C., Kulla, M. (1996). On the relationship between mobbing factors, and job content, social work environment, and health outcomes. *European Journal of Work and Organizational Psychology, 5*(2), 215-237.

About the Authors

Catherine M. Mattice, MA, is President of Civility Partners, LLC, a professional training and consulting firm that specializes in providing universal solutions for negative behaviors in the workplace. Through her consulting, coaching and training programs, she assists her clients in designing and realizing positive corporate cultures. She believes eradicating negative behaviors goes beyond removing them, and requires a focus on building a positive and civil workplace in order to make sustainable and preventative changes.

As a subject matter expert on the topic of workplace bullying, Catherine has published several articles in the areas of human resources, personal development, conflict resolution, and business management. Some of her favorite publications include a featured cover article in *HR Times Magazine*, "The Bully-Free Workplace"; and an article published alongside Howard Putnam, former CEO of Southwest Airlines, in *Personal Development Magazine*. She has also been cited in USA Today, MSNBC, and the Huffington Post as an expert, as well as appeared on news stations such as FOX, NBC, and ABC nationwide. Catherine has also presented her academic research and corporate training programs on the topic of bullying both nationally and internationally.

Catherine is active in the International Association for Workplace Bullying & Harassment (IAWBH) and is Past-President of the American Society of Training & Development (ASTD), San Diego Chapter. She is also an adjunct professor at National University and Southwestern College, and received her bachelor's and master's degrees in communication from San Diego State University.

Visit Catherine's educational website on the topic of workplace bullying at www.NoWorkplaceBullies.com. Visit her consulting firm's website for more information about her services at www.CivilityPartners.com. Feel free to email her at Catherine@CivilityPartners.com.

E G Sebastian, CPC, is an international speaker, who speaks six languages, and presents extensively on behavior and personality related topics, such as conflict management, effective communication, dealing with difficult people, and dealing with bullying.

E.G. loves to study what makes people tick - what motivates them, what are their fears, what triggers conflict and how to manage it best, how to recognize and best communicate with different personality types, and how to build successful relationships based on this knowledge. He loves to "Wow!" his audience members with the simplicity of understanding and "reading" different personality styles, and the ease of co-existing with different styles once one understands what makes each personality style tick.

E.G. believes that communication and good people skills are the most important skills that one can master. Only with mastery of these skills can one attain true success in both personal and professional life; therefore, most of E.G.'s presentations focus to a great extent on helping his audiences better understand basic human behavior and building better interpersonal skills based on that understanding.

During the past decade, E.G. collected and laid out his findings on improving personal relationships and improving productivity in his book, *Communication Skills Magic – Improve Your*

Relationship & Productivity through Better Understanding Your Personality Style and the Personality Styles of Those Around You (2009). You can download the first few chapter of the book at www.CommunicationSkillsMagic.com.

To inquire about E.G.'s availability to present at your next event, or for more info on his programs, please contact him at StopBullying@egSebastian.com, or Toll FREE at 877-379-3793. Learn more about E.G. at his website: http://www.StopThatBully.com.

Contributor, **Patricia G. Barnes, JD**, is an appellate judge, attorney, author, and legal expert on workplace bullying. Her experience in both employment and domestic violence law led her to observe the similarities between abuse in the home and in the workplace, and to see that many employment lawsuits reflect underlying workplace bullying. Ms. Barnes created and moderates a legal blog on workplace abuse (http://abusergoestowork.com) and has written about workplace bullying for various publications. A resident of Reno, NV, she is also the author of two legal reference books for CQ Press, and she edited a three-volume series on domestic violence for Garland Publishing, Inc.

Contributor, **Kathleen Bartle, MA** (www.kathleenbartle.com) is a consultant on workplace conflict to executives in the U.S. and worldwide. Her work helps organizations reduce the billions of dollars workplace conflict costs.

Kathleen's clients have been in strategic positions in business, government, and non-profit and research environments. Because of her years in academia and science, she understands the unique problems in academia and science where competition fosters destructive and expensive conflict.

She designs unique training programs for leaders. She is committed to the best interests of her clients and has the unique ability to determine the most cost-effective and long-term solutions for them.

36589147R00141

Made in the USA
San Bernardino, CA
27 July 2016